# PRESIDENTS
# OF THE UNITED STATES

*Below: The White House, Washington, D.C.,*
*the executive mansion of the President.*
*The site was chosen by President Washington and*
*the building was designed by James Hoban. It was*
*restored after being burned by the British in 1814.*
*At that time, the smoke-stained walls were painted*
*white, giving rise to the title "White House."*
*The grounds (about 18 acres) were designed*
*by Andrew Jackson Downing.*

*Right: The Washington Monument, Washington, D.C., designed by Robert Mills. The shaft is composed of blocks of stone from the various states, some foreign governments, and private individuals. The cornerstone was laid on July 4, 1848, but the base was not completed until 1880. The aluminum tip was put in place in 1884, and the Monument was dedicated the following year. It was opened to the public in 1888.*

# Index

*The Mount Rushmore National Memorial, in the Black Hills northeast of Custer, South Dakota. The colossal busts are of Presidents Washington, Jefferson, Lincoln, and Theodore Roosevelt. The Memorial was authorized by Congress in 1925, Gutzon Borglum being selected as sculptor. The work was nearly finished when he died in 1941 and was completed later in that year by his son Lincoln Borglum.*

*Overleaf: The Capitol of the United States, Washington, D.C. The site was chosen by President Washington in consultation with Major Pierre Charles L'Enfant. In 1792 William Thornton was appointed architect and Washington laid the cornerstone the following year. Later E. S. Hallet, George Hadfield, and James Hoban worked on the building. In 1814 the uncompleted Capitol was burned by the British; its restoration was undertaken by B. H. Latrobe. He was succeeded in 1818 by Charles Bulfinch, who completed the design in 1830. The building was greatly enlarged from 1851 to 1865 by T. U. Walter, who added the House and Senate wings and the dome.*

# PRESIDENTS
# UNITED

GOLDEN PRESS · NEW YORK

Western Publishing Company, Inc.
Racine, Wisconsin

# of the
# STATES

CORNEL ADAM LENGYEL

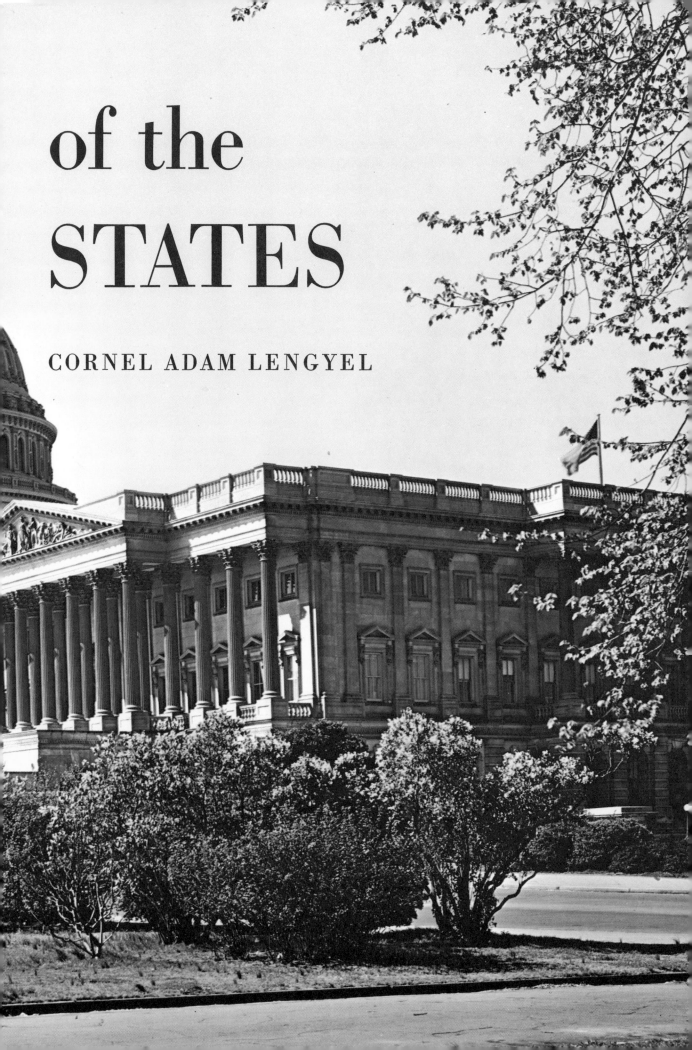

Also by Cornel Adam Lengyel:
*Four Days in July*

With the exception of the items listed below, the pictorial material in this book is from the Collections of the Library of Congress. The publisher wishes to thank the staff of the Prints and Photographs Division of the Library, especially Mr. Milton Kaplan, for their assistance and co-operation in assembling this material. The daguerreotypes and photographs on the pages listed below are from the Brady-Handy Collection in the Library of Congress and are used through the courtesy of Mrs. Alice Handy Cox and Mr. Frederick Cox: 25 (top), 32 (top), 37, 44, 48 (top), 56, 58 (left), 61 (top), 63 (top), 70 (left), 74.

The photographs on pages 2, 3, 6 and 7 were taken by Mr. Theodor Horydczak and are used through the courtesy of the Davis Studio, Washington, D.C.

The illustration on page 9 is from the Bureau of Engraving and Printing of the U.S. Treasury department.

OTHER PHOTO CREDITS: Lawrence L. Smith from Photo Researchers, Inc., 5; The Metropolitan Museum of Art, Bequest of Charles Allen Munn, 1924, 10; The White House Collection, 11, 38 (right), 71 (right); courtesy, Museum of Fine Arts, Boston, 12; National Gallery of Art, Washington, D.C., Mellon Collection, 14; Independence National Historical Park Collection, 15 (top), 18 (top left); courtesy, The Society for Preservation of New England Antiquities, 15 (bottom); courtesy, The Architect of the Capitol, 18-19; American Scenic and Historic Preservation Society, photograph by Louis H. Frohman, 21; courtesy, The Art Commission of the City of New York, photograph by Taylor and Dull, New York, 23; The New York Public Library Picture Collection, 27, 52 (top left), 66 (top); The Ladies' Hermitage Association, 28 (bottom); The Essex Institute, 35; courtesy, Harry Shaw Newman, The Old Print Shop, New York City, 36, 39 (bottom), photograph by Louis H. Frohman; Buffalo and Erie County Historical Society, 45 (bottom); The Smithsonian Institution, National Collection of Fine Arts, 48 (bottom); McLellan Lincoln Collection, John Hay Library, Brown University, 55; Culver Pictures, Inc., 69, 75 (top); American Museum of Natural History, 76; U.S. Signal Corps photo, No. 111-SC-61128 in the National Archives, 81; Brown Brothers, 83 (bottom); Franklin D. Roosevelt Library, Hyde Park, New York, 88 (bottom), 89; United Press International Photo, 90, 91, 93 (top), 94, 95 (bottom), 96, 97, 100, 101, 102 (top); U.S. Army photograph, 93 (bottom); Harris & Ewing from Gilloon Photo Agency, 95 (top); The White House Press Secretary, 98 (bottom); Wide World Photos, 99, 104, 105, 106, 107, 108.

The text of this book was adapted from
PRESIDENTS OF THE U.S.A.: Profiles and Pictures
Published by arrangement with Bantam Books, Inc.
Copyright © 1961, by Bantam Books, Inc.
All rights reserved.

*Seventh Printing, 1977*

*Mount Vernon, the home of President Washington*

# CONTENTS

*A portrait of Washington by the Swedish artist Adolf Ulric Wertmüller, done when Washington was 62 years old.*

# George Washington

**Born:** *February 22, 1732, Pope's Creek, near Fredericksburg, Westmoreland County, Virginia.*
**Parents:** *Augustine and Mary Ball Washington.*
**Education:** *private.* **Married:** *1759, Mrs. Martha Dandridge Custis (1731-1802), two stepchildren.*
**Career:** *surveyor; farmer; soldier; member, Virginia house of burgesses, 1759-74; member, Continental Congress, 1774-75; commander-in-chief, Continental Army, 1775-83; president, Constitutional Convention, 1787; first president, 1789-97.*
**Died:** *December 14, 1799, Mount Vernon, Virginia.*

Whether engraved on a postage stamp or carved on a mountainside his calm and lofty expression is known to every American. A New World hero to match the best of Greece or Rome, his character and deeds are familiar to lovers of freedom around the globe. "First in war, first in peace, first in the hearts of his countrymen," Washington led the revolutionary army during America's desperate struggle for independence. He freed the colonies, unified the first people's republic, helped mold its enduring Constitution. As president of the new United States, he set the high first example in governing a free people. Greatest of great Americans, he has become an almost legendary figure. Yet, as Abigail Adams, who knew him for a quarter of a century, observed: "Simple truth is his best, his greatest eulogy."

Born on the family farm in Virginia, between the Potomac and the Rappahannock Rivers, young Washington was raised on lands which his great-grandfather, a native of England, had settled. When the boy was 11, his father died. His widowed mother, hard pressed to support a family of five children, could not send George to college. At 15, a sturdy lad who excelled in mathematics, he became a surveyor. His first big job was to survey the estate of his neighbor, Lord Fairfax, whose royal grant of six million acres ran from the Atlantic seaboard to the Alleghenies.

The youth spent months in the uncharted wilderness. He learned to rough it, as he learned to love the vast and beautiful Shenandoah Valley and the Blue Ridge Mountains. His self-reliant spirit was strengthened by his experiences in the hardship school of the pioneers. "I have not slept above three nights or four in a bed," he wrote home, "but after walking all day, I lay down before the fire upon a little hay, straw fodder, or bear skin, with man, wife, and children, like a parcel of dogs or cats, and happy is he who gets the berth nearest the fire . . ."

At 20, after a trip to the West Indies, Washington was commissioned in the militia to guard Virginia's frontiers against French and Indian raiders. A tall powerful youth, six feet three, with a long nose and a pock-marked face, he wrote to Governor Dinwiddie applying for a dangerous mission, "I have a constitution hardy enough to undergo the most severe threats." Carrying a message of warning to the French officer at Fort Le Boeuf, he crossed the Alleghenies in the dress of an Indian scout. In the middle of winter he made his way through a wilderness of bears and rattlesnakes, built rafts to ford icy streams, delivered his message, and returned the way he came.

For three years he took part in the French and Indian War. When he saw the results of a massacre at Fort Necessity, he exclaimed, "If dying would glut the Indians' revenge, I would be a willing offering to savage fury and die by inches to save a people!"

While serving under General Braddock, the 23-year-old Washington tried to advise him on frontier fighting, but the stubborn British commander scorned the young colonial's advice. Trapped in an ambush on the banks of the Monongahela in July, 1755, the British and colonial troops were nearly wiped out.

*Martha Washington, painted in 1878 by Eliphalet F. Andrews. The portrait now hangs in the White House.*

*A highly romanticized painting of Washington at the Passing of the Delaware, done by Thomas Sully in 1819.*

Braddock himself was killed. Two horses were shot from under Washington and four bullets passed through his coat. Plunging into the forest, Washington barely escaped with his life. Later, he wrote to his brother from Fort Cumberland: "As I have heard, since my arrival in this place, a circumstantial account of my death and dying speech, I take this early opportunity of contradicting both . . ."

Elected to the Virginia legislature, he was praised for his bravery in the field. When he rose to a burst of cheers, he found he could not speak; so, blushing, he sat in awkward silence. "Your modesty is equal to your valor," the Speaker observed. "And both are beyond the power of words."

At 27, Washington married Martha Custis, a young widow with two small children. Managing his farms— he had inherited Mount Vernon, his holdings were increased by his wife's estate, and in time his farms and woodlands covered 70,000 acres—he was active in the open from dawn to sunset. Paying attention to the smallest details, he became one of the best farmers in the country. He could fell a tree like a lumberjack, work iron like a blacksmith, shape wood with the skill of a carpenter. He sold flour from his mills and tobacco from his drying sheds, raised horses in his stables, and went fox-hunting in his woods. He enjoyed attending balls in Williamsburg and often entertained guests at Mount Vernon.

After 1770, opposed to the Stamp Act and other unjust measures passed by the British parliament, Washington became prominent in the resistance movement, with Patrick Henry, George Mason, Thomas Jefferson and other gentlemen in Virginia. When the port of Boston was closed by King George III in an effort to starve out the New England rebels, Washington said, "I will raise a thousand men, at my own expense, and march them to the relief of Boston."

In the spring of 1775 he attended the great protest meeting of colonial leaders, the Continental Congress in Philadelphia. While his fellow delegates were still drafting petitions to George III, Washington appeared in his blue and buff colonel's uniform of the Virginia militia. This was his way of saying, "The time has come to fight for our rights."

When John Adams nominated him as commander of the people's army, Washington was reluctant to accept. When the delegates elected him unanimously, he thanked them for the great honor. He would serve without a salary, he said, but was anxious to forewarn them: "I do not think myself equal to the command I am honored with." The same evening, discussing his appointment with a fellow delegate, Patrick Henry, he told him with tears in his eyes: "Remember, Mr. Henry, what I now tell you. From the day I enter upon the command of the American armies, I date the fall and the ruin of my reputation."

On his way north to take over his command, he learned of the Battle of Bunker Hill. "Did the militia fight?" he asked. "Yes!" he was told. "Then the liberties of the country are safe." He took command of the camp at Cambridge, Massachusetts, on July 3, 1775. He raised the siege of Boston. A week before the Declaration of Independence was adopted in Philadelphia, he spoke to his ill-equipped army of farm boys in the port of New York. They were within sight of an enemy armada of nearly five hundred British warships. "The time is now near at hand which must probably determine whether Americans are to be free men or slaves. The fate of unborn millions will now depend upon the courage and conduct of this army. . . . Let us therefore rely upon the goodness of the cause . . . to animate and encourage us to great and noble actions."

For seven long and bitter years Washington held together his rag, tag, and bobtail army against the most unequal odds, against cold and starvation, against 30,000 mercenaries from abroad, against neglect and treachery at home. From Valley Forge to Yorktown, his indomitable will and strength of character maintained a much-reduced army and upheld a nearly lost cause, a cause he had pledged himself to defend. "Our cause is noble," he said. "It is the cause of all mankind."

Finally, after many reversals, and with the help of the French fleet, he forced Cornwallis to surrender at Yorktown on October 19, 1781. The American rebellion had become a successful revolution; the people of the colonies had won the right to form a government of their own choosing. Bidding farewell to his soldiers before returning to his long-neglected farms by the Potomac, Washington remarked with feeling, "How much more delightful the task of making improvements on the earth than all the vainglory which can be acquired from ravaging it!"

After a turbulent period of trial, the Articles of Confederation, which had been adopted by the Continental Congress, proved ineffectual as a basis for union. The leaders of the 13 newly independent and nearly sovereign states met in Philadelphia to draft a new constitution, one which would give more authority to the federal government. In May of 1787, Washington was asked to preside over a Constitutional Convention. During the weeks of debate, when passions ran high, Washington reminded his much-divided colleagues of the great object before them: to form a more perfect union. "Let us raise a standard to which the wise and honest can repair," he said. "The event is in the hands of God."

Under Washington's guidance the great instrument was hammered out—the present Constitution of the United States—with its remarkable system of checks and balances to prevent any one man or party or branch of the government from gaining too much power; with its Bill of Rights to protect the hard-won freedoms of the individual against oppression by the state; with its provision for amendments whereby the changing needs of future generations could be met by new accommodations in the laws of the land.

Though Washington longed to return to Mount Vernon, the graying hero, now 57, was persuaded to serve as the country's first president. When zealous men wanted to crown him King of America, he dismissed them with scorn: "If you have any regard for your country or respect for me, banish forever these thoughts from your mind!" Some wanted to address him with the resounding title "His Most Gracious Highness, President of the United States and Protector of Their Liberties." The accepted title became "Mr. President."

From a balcony of the City Hall in New York, the new nation's temporary capital, Washington took the first presidential oath of office on April 30, 1789: "I do solemnly swear that I will faithfully execute the office of President of the United States, and will, to the best of my ability, preserve, protect, and defend the Constitution of the United States."

In his first inaugural address he spoke of America's mission: "The preservation of the sacred fire of liberty and the destiny of the republican model of government are justly considered as deeply, and perhaps as finally, staked on the experiment entrusted to the hands of the American people."

Launching the revolutionary experiment, the republic trembled at first in a conflict of principles. But Washington, true heir of the Enlightenment, held firmly to the larger vision. Above party spirit, he drew

*The first Presidential Mansion, at No. 1 Cherry Street in New York City, the first U.S. capital (1789-90).*

the most able men into his cabinet, men as diverse in views as Alexander Hamilton and Thomas Jefferson. He did all he could to unify the country, to give dignity and strength to the people's government both at home and abroad.

Without prejudice of any kind, in his *Message to Catholics* he said: "I hope ever to see America foremost among nations in example of justice and liberality." To the Quakers in Philadelphia: "The liberty of conscience enjoyed by these states . . . is not only among the choicest of their *blessings* but also of their *rights.*" To the Jewish Congregation in Newport: "May the children of the stock of Abraham . . . enjoy the good will of the other inhabitants . . . for happily the government of the United States gives to bigotry no sanction, to persecution no assistance."

Having served two terms, Washington refused a third. He considered it dangerous to keep any one man in the highest office too long. He was eager to retire to Mount Vernon. In his Farewell Address, which is read each year in Congress, he gave his best parting counsel to a country he had served with selfless dedication.

"My first wish is to see this plague of mankind—war—banished from the earth," he said. He urged the people "to guard against the impostures of pretended patriotism," to frown upon "the first dawning of every attempt to alienate any portion of our country from the rest." Some day, he predicted, "taking its pattern from the United States, there will be founded a United States of Europe." Meanwhile, America must follow its own independent course. "Observe good faith and justice toward all nations, cultivate peace and harmony with all. . . . Steer clear of permanent alliances with any portion of the foreign world."

One of Washington's closest and keenest-eyed observers, Jefferson, recorded: "His mind was great and powerful. . . . His integrity was most pure, his justice the most inflexible I have ever known, no motives of interest or consanguinity, of friendship or hatred, being able to bias his decision. He was indeed in every sense of the words, a wise, a good, and a great man. . . . Of his career, the history of the world furnishes no other example."

For new and future generations, the tall stone shaft in the nation's capital, named in his honor, remains a permanent reminder: WASHINGTON, THE BRAVE, THE WISE, THE GOOD, SUPREME IN WAR, IN COUNCIL, AND IN PEACE, VALIANT WITHOUT AMBITION, DISCREET WITHOUT FEAR . . . THE FATHER OF NATIONS, THE FRIEND OF MANKIND . . .

*General and Mrs. Washington with her grandchildren, George and Eleanor Custis. Painted, 1796, by Edward Savage.*

# John Adams

**Born:** *October 30, 1735, Braintree (now Quincy), Massachusetts.* **Parents:** *John and Susanna Boylston Adams.* **Education:** *Harvard, 1755.* **Married:** *1764, Abigail Smith (1744-1818), five children.* **Career:** *teacher; lawyer; member, Continental Congress, 1774-78; commissioner to France, 1778; member, Massachusetts constitutional conventions, 1779, 1820; minister to the Netherlands, 1780; envoy to Great Britain, 1785-88; vice-president, 1789-97; second president, 1797-1801.* **Died:** *July 4, 1826, Quincy, Mass.*

Son of a small yeoman farmer, John Adams left the village of Braintree at 16 to enter Harvard College. At the time Harvard had a faculty of half a dozen scholars and some 30 students. A short, stocky lad, young Adams was undecided whether to study to be a physician, a surgeon, or a clergyman. He took part

in school readings of Shakespeare and was admired for his dramatic power in rendering speeches from *Coriolanus*. Graduating with a bachelor of arts degree, he delivered the commencement oration in Latin, a feat which won for him his first job: teaching Latin in nearby Worcester's one-room country school house.

"My little school, like the great world, is made up of kings, politicians, divines," 20-year-old Adams recorded in his diary. "Fops, buffoons, sycophants, fools . . . and every other character I see in the world . . . I had rather sit in school to see which of my pupils will turn out a hero and which a rake, which a philosopher and which a parasite, than have 20 waistcoats and a thousand pounds a year."

While teaching he studied law and was admitted to the Boston bar in 1758. Known for his honesty, courage, and brilliant legal abilities, he became a successful lawyer and was offered profitable posts as attorney for the Crown. Adams turned down the offers. Opposed to the Stamp Act, he argued against taxation without representation before the royal governor. With his cousin, Samuel Adams, and John Hancock, he became a leader of the independence movement.

On March 5, 1770, British soldiers, quartered in Boston, fired into a crowd of rioters, killing five men. Though popular feeling ran high, though Adams had much to lose and nothing to gain, he agreed to defend Captain Prescott, the British officer involved in the "Boston Massacre." Through his able defense he

*Mrs. John Adams, painted by Gilbert Stuart about 1812. She was the wife of one president and mother of another.*

won the officer's acquittal. "Facts are stubborn things," he told the jury. "And whatever may be our wishes, our inclinations, or the dictates of our passion, they cannot alter the state of facts and evidence." The act, characteristic of Adams, alienated many of his supporters.

Soon after the Boston Tea Party, when the port was blockaded by the Royal Navy, Adams left for Philadelphia to attend the Continental Congress, the illegal first parliament of America. "Politics are an ordeal path among red-hot plowshares," he told his beloved wife Abigail when he left. "Who would then be a politician for the sake of running about barefoot among them? Yet somebody must!"

In the Congress he sat on more committees and did more work than any other delegate. The bold measures he proposed to pave the way to independence alarmed or offended many of his colleagues. After the battle at Lexington he urged that Washington be made commander of the people's army. When a declaration for independence was about to be drafted, he insisted that Jefferson write the draft. In answer to modest Jefferson's objections, the sharp-eyed New Englander gave his reasons. "Reason first: you are a Virginian, and a Virginian ought to appear at the head of this business. Reason second: I am obnoxious, suspected, unpopular. You are very much otherwise. Reason third: you can write 10 times better than I can."

During the heated debates that preceded the adoption of the Declaration of Independence, Adams fought for the measure, "for every word of it," and was known as the Colossus of the Debates, the Atlas of Independence. Shortly before July 4, 1776, he closed one speech in a way that moved his colleagues out of their seats:

"All that I have, all that I am, all that I hope for in this life, I stake on our cause," cried Adams. "For me the die is cast. Sink or swim, live or die, to survive or perish with my country is my unalterable resolution!" Due in great part to his energy and conviction, the great Declaration was driven through the divided Congress.

During his difficult years in Philadelphia he wrote a remarkable series of *Familiar Letters* to his devoted wife Abigail, who was trying to maintain the family on the farm at Braintree. Adams revealed to her his innermost thoughts and anxieties. Concerned with his children's future, he exhorted his wife not to neglect their education. "John Quincy has genius," he wrote of his eight-year-old son. "And so has Charles. Take care that they don't go astray. Fix their attention on great and glorious objects. Root out every little thing. Weed out every meanness. Make them great and manly. Teach them to scorn injustice, ingratitude, cowardice and falsehood. Let them revere nothing but religion, morality, and liberty!"

Sent to France by Congress in 1778, Adams negotiated loans for the hard-pressed colonies. From Holland he raised a loan of two million dollars. On one of his missions across the blockaded Atlantic, he took

*The Adamses were the first presidential family to live in the White House, then uncompleted. Mrs. Adams made a drying room out of the audience room. The drawing below shows the winning design by the architect James Hoban.*

*The U.S. Capitol as it looked when Adams was president. At that time Washington had a population of only 3,210.*

his sons with him. Shipwrecked off the coast of Spain, they were three months on the road to Paris. "The boys have had a chance to learn Spanish," was Adams' comment on the ordeal.

After the Revolution, he negotiated the Treaty of Peace with Great Britain. As minister to England in 1785, he was the first independent American to stand before the throne and face a resentful George III. Returning home he served as vice-president for two terms. When Washington retired in 1796, John Adams was elected president—by a majority of three electoral votes.

Always a crotchety non-conformist, he was soon at odds with his cabinet and with his party and its leader, Alexander Hamilton. Horrified by the excesses of the French Revolution, he lost his faith in the common sense of the people. He feared the tyranny of both the majority and the minority; he distrusted the rising tide of Jeffersonian democracy. He prevented America from joining France in a war against England.

To gag political agitators from abroad and to stop public criticism of his administration, he approved the Alien and Sedition Acts. A violation of the Bill of Rights, curtailing freedom of speech and freedom of the press, the acts raised a storm of protest and completed his break with both Hamilton and Jefferson. For his own epitaph he proudly composed the line: "Here lies John Adams, who took upon himself the responsibility of the peace with France, in the year 1800."

A Puritan farmer's son who became a self-made aristocrat, he did his duty as he saw it and never lost his talent for making enemies. When his character was bitterly attacked, he said, "Let them spit their venom and hiss like serpents. . . . For more than fifty years I have lived in an enemy country." Failing to be re-elected, he retired to Braintree at 65. A life-long scholar, he had few illusions about human nature. His countrymen would forget his great labors on their behalf. "The history of our Revolution will be one continuous lie from one end to the other," he remarked in one of his savagely honest and zestful moods. "The essence of the whole will be that Doctor Franklin's electrical rod smote the earth and out sprang General Washington. Then Franklin electrified him with his rod and thenceforth these two conducted all the policies, negotiations, legislatures and war."

At 90, Adams lay on his deathbed in the farmhouse at Braintree. He had lived long enough to see his son, John Quincy, become the sixth president of the United States. When a village committee called on the dying man and asked for a toast for the Fourth of July celebration, Adams said, "I give you: 'Independence Forever!' " He died on July 4, 1826, the same day Jefferson died at Monticello. His reported last words were: "Thomas Jefferson still survives . . ."

# Thomas Jefferson

**Born:** *April 13, 1743, Shadwell, Goochland (now Albemarle) County, Virginia.* **Parents:** *Peter and Jane Randolph Jefferson.* **Education:** *William and Mary, 1760-62.* **Married:** *1772, Mrs. Martha Wayles Skelton (1748-82), six children.* **Career:** *farmer; lawyer; member, Virginia house of burgesses, 1769-74; member, Continental Congress, 1775-76, 1783-85; member, Virginia house of delegates, 1776-79; 1781; governor of Virginia, 1779-81; minister to France, 1785-89; secretary of state, 1789-93; vice-president, 1797-1801; third president, 1801-09; founded University of Virginia, chartered 1819.* **Died:** *July 4, 1826, Monticello, near Charlottesville, Virginia.*

"We hold these truths to be self-evident: that all men are created equal, that they are endowed by their Creator with certain inalienable rights, that among these are life, liberty, and the pursuit of happiness . . ."

At the time Jefferson wrote the revolutionary manifesto, in a bricklayer's house in Philadelphia, the 33-year-old author of the Declaration of Independence was a delegate from Virginia to the Continental Congress. A lanky, red-headed provincial lawyer, six feet tall, he had the strong build of a frontiersman and the fine bold head of an aristocrat.

Though he had never traveled more than four hundred miles beyond his birthplace in the Blue Ridge Mountains, he spoke six languages; he could read Homer and Virgil in the original; he could also "calculate an eclipse, survey an estate, tie an artery, plan an edifice, try a cause, break a horse, dance a minuet, play the violin."

One of the most versatile men in history, Jefferson took all knowledge for his province. Nothing that was human was alien to him. Wherever he turned his many-faceted mind he sought to bring fresh light, to add to man's freedom and understanding.

His father, Peter Jefferson, a surveyor and farmer of legendary strength, died when the boy was 14. His mother was left with eight children. At 17, young

*John Trumbull's painting of the signing of the Declaration of Independence. It hangs in the Capitol.*

Jefferson rode from the family farm near Monticello to attend the College of William and Mary.

The self-reliant youth found challenging pursuits in mathematics, music, and architecture. Studying law, he spent five years in George Wythe's office; he prepared more than a thousand legal cases. Later, to his close friends and disciples, Madison and Monroe—two future presidents whose characters he molded—he recommended his own schedule as a student: "From daybreak till eight in the morning, study the natural sciences. From eight to twelve, read law. From twelve to one, read politics. In the afternoon read history and the Bible. From dark to bedtime, literature, criticism, classic oratory."

At 28, Jefferson married beautiful Martha Skelton. On January 1, 1772, in the midst of a blizzard, he carried his bride across the threshold of their half-finished home at Monticello. When duty called him, he tore himself from his beloved family, his farm, his books, and left for the assembly of rebels in Philadelphia.

Not an orator, Jefferson hardly spoke two words in the Continental Congress. But his "peculiar felicity of expression" as a writer and thinker was known to some of the delegates. Because of this, he was put on a committee with John Adams, Benjamin Franklin, Robert R. Livingston and Roger Sherman to draft the decisive first public statement of the Congress: the Declaration of Independence.

Parts of Jefferson's draft were bitterly debated by some of the delegates in Philadelphia, while the huge British armada was already landing in New York less than ninety miles away. Due to the objections of two colonies, South Carolina and Georgia, the passages which outlawed Negro slavery were cut. Had they not been, the Civil War might have been averted. "However, the thing in its nature is so good," said Richard Henry Lee, author of the original resolution for independence, "that no cookery can spoil the dish for the palates of free men!" On July 4, 1776, the Declaration was adopted.

In 1779, during the Revolution, Jefferson became governor of Virginia. In the war-torn state, repeatedly invaded by the enemy, he carried out important reforms. Feudal laws of inheritance were abolished. Free education and public libraries were introduced. The Statute of Virginia for Religious Freedom was designed to protect all citizens in their freedom of conscience and to eliminate forever the dangers of religious bigotry and persecution. Jefferson intended "to comprehend within the mantle of its protection the Jew and the Gentile, the Christian and Mohammedan and infidel of every description."

Appointed minister to France, succeeding his good friend Franklin, he spent five intensely active years in Europe. His counsel was sought by all who hoped to emulate America's example in securing the rights of man. His book *Notes on Virginia,* published in Paris, spread his fame as a scholar.

Returning home on the eve of the French Revolution, he was appointed secretary of state by President Washington. Elected vice-president in 1796, he became leader of the opposition to the Federalist party. The presidential vote in 1800 resulted in a tie between Jefferson and Aaron Burr, each having received 73 electoral votes. The tie was broken when Hamilton decided to throw the Federalist votes to Jefferson.

President Jefferson pushed through the Louisiana Purchase, buying from Napoleon for 16 million dollars a tract which ran from the Mississippi to the Rocky Mountains—a real estate bargain at three cents an acre. In effect, he more than doubled the size of the country, without shedding a drop of blood. He opened up millions of new acres to settlers in the West. "The earth belongs to the living," said Jefferson. Partly at his own expense, he launched the Lewis and Clark expedition to explore the Northwest, a survey called "incomparably the most perfect achievement of its kind in the history of the world."

Re-elected in 1804 by an overwhelming majority, he sought to keep America from becoming embroiled in the Napoleonic wars in Europe. He did so by putting an embargo on shipping. This made him unpopular with Yankee shippers and with the "war hawks" who were clamoring for action against Great Britain.

When he left the White House, "with hands as clean as they are empty," he retired to Monticello, where he had designed and built one of the most beautiful homes in America. A widower—his wife had died in 1782—he devoted his last years to realizing a lifelong dream: the founding of the University of Virginia. He wanted the University to be a school where the youth of the New World could pursue "the illimitable freedom of the human mind." Laboring under increasing financial strain, the Sage of Monticello completed the huge task when he was nearly 80 and close to bankruptcy. On the entrance to the university he set the motto: "You shall know the truth and the truth shall set you free."

An uncommon man, Jefferson had abiding faith in the common people. He wanted to extend the area of freedom, to give more and more men a chance to become uncommon. "There is a natural aristocracy among men," he wrote to John Adams after their reconciliation. "The grounds of this are virtue and talent. The natural aristocracy I consider the most precious gift of nature, for the instruction, the trusts, the government of society . . ."

Invited by the mayor of Washington in 1826 to partake in the fiftieth celebration of Independence Day, the 83-year-old survivor was too ill to attend the festivities. In what was to be his last letter he thanked the mayor and wrote of his hopes for the Declaration of Independence:

"May it be to the world what I believe it will be (to some parts sooner, to others later, but finally to all), the signal for arousing man to burst the chains. . . . All eyes are opened or opening to the rights of man. . . . The mass of mankind has not been born with saddles on their backs, nor a favored few, booted and spurred, ready to ride them legitimately, by the grace of God. These are grounds of hope for others. . . ."

Jefferson died at Monticello on July 4, 1826. For his epitaph he listed three things for which he hoped to be remembered "as testimonials that I have lived":

*Here was buried*
*THOMAS JEFFERSON*
*Author of the Declaration of American Independence*
*of the Statute of Virginia for Religious Freedom*
*and Father of the University of Virginia*

*Monticello, the home of Jefferson. A self-taught architect, he designed his house. Building began in 1770.*

# James Madison

**Born:** *March 16, 1751, Port Conway, King George County, Virginia.* **Parents:** *James and Eleanor Rose Conway Madison.* **Education:** *College of New Jersey (now Princeton), 1771.* **Married:** *1794, Mrs. Dorothea (Dolly) Payne Todd (1768-1849), one stepson.* **Career:** *farmer; lawyer; member, Virginia constitutional convention; 1776-77; member, Virginia council of state, 1778-79; member, Continental Congress, 1780-83, 1786-88; member, Virginia house of delegates, 1784-86; member, Constitutional Convention, 1787; U.S. representative, 1789-97; secretary of state, 1801-9; fourth president, 1809-17; rector, University of Virginia, 1826-36; member, Virginia constitutional convention, 1829.* **Died:** *June 28, 1836, Montpellier (now spelled Montpelier), Orange County, Virginia.*

As a child, James Madison was a frail, shy, studious boy, below average in size. He was tutored at home by a Scottish schoolmaster; he studied Latin, Greek, French, and Spanish. At 18, he left the family farm at Montpelier, Virginia, to enter the College of New Jersey at Princeton. A hard-working student, for months he slept only three hours a day. In 1772, he studied Hebrew and theology with Reverend John Witherspoon, subsequently a signer of the Declaration of Independence.

At 25, as a member of the Virginia legislature, Madison supported Jefferson's reform program. He sought to abolish slavery. He helped to draft the Virginia Plan, which had a strong influence in shaping the Constitution of the United States.

At 36, as a member of the Constitutional Convention, Madison sat by Chairman Washington's table in the State House in Philadelphia and took shorthand notes of the proceedings. His reports form an eye-witness account of an event important in man's political evolution.

Madison took the lead in framing the Constitution and in urging its adoption by the states. Though honored as the Father of the Constitution, he himself was too modest to accept such a title. "You give me a credit to which I have no claim," he wrote in a letter two years before he died. The Constitution was not, he explained, "the offspring of a single brain." It was "the work of many heads and many hands." Jefferson called the Constitution "the result of the collected wisdom of our country." Yet more than any other single delegate, Madison labored to shape and sustain it.

In favor of a strong central government, he sought to prevent the abuse of power, to protect the citizens of the new nation both from each other and from their officials. He believed that a carefully designed system of checks and balances would assure a more equal distribution of power in government. He felt that the more widely power was spread, the better chance there was to safeguard the rights and freedoms of the individual.

To support his views, Madison contributed to *The Federalist,* a series of essays supporting the new Constitution. Fifty years before Karl Marx, he stated that the most common source of friction in society is "the unequal distribution of property." Madison said: "Those who hold and those who are without property have ever formed distinct interests in society. The regulation of these various and conflicting interests forms the principal task of modern legislation."

Madison fought to add the Bill of Rights to the Constitution. It appears in the great charter as the first ten amendments, to guarantee to every American, among other important rights: *Freedom of speech . . . Freedom of the press . . . Freedom of religion . . . The right to peaceful assembly . . . The right* to petition the government . . . The right to fair trial.

As a bachelor of 43, James Madison met and wooed Dolly Payne Todd in 1794. An attractive young widow of 26, Dolly was the daughter of the landlady of a Philadelphia boarding house. When Madison entered the White House in 1809, Dolly became a popular hostess, known for her gala parties.

"Mrs. Madison is a fine, portly, buxom dame who has a smile and a pleasant word for everybody," reported Washington Irving. "But as for Jemmy Madison—ah, poor Jemmy! He is but a withered little apple-John!" In appearance the least commanding of chief executives, Madison, five feet four, never weighed more than a hundred pounds.

During his administration, increasing friction with the British over the freedom of the seas led to the War of 1812. In one surprising raid on Washington, British marines set fire to public buildings and burned down the White House. Madison and his wife were obliged to escape into the Virginia woods. Criticized for America's lack of defense preparations, Madison regained his prestige with the report of the great victory at New Orleans, where Andrew Jackson had driven off the invaders.

Retiring from the White House in 1817, Madison returned to Montpelier. Once a frail sickly child, he outlived all the other founders of the republic. On Jefferson's death, he became rector of the University of Virginia. He died in 1836, at the age of 85.

*The great event of Madison's administration was the War of 1812. The final victory for the Americans took place at New Orleans. A peace treaty had been signed two weeks before, but the news had not yet reached the United States.*

# James Monroe

**Born:** *April 28, 1758, Westmoreland County, Virginia.* **Parents:** *Spence and Elizabeth Jones Monroe.* **Education:** *William and Mary, 1776.* **Married:** *1786, Elizabeth Kortright (1768-1830), three children.* **Career:** *farmer; lawyer; officer, Continental Army, 1775-80; member, Virginia house of delegates, 1782, 1787; member, Continental Congress, 1783-86; delegate, Virginia constitutional convention, 1788; U.S. senator, 1790-94; minister to France, 1794-96; governor of Virginia, 1799-1803, 1811; envoy to France, January to July, 1803; minister to Great Britain, 1803-07; member, Virginia assembly, 1810-11; secretary of state, 1811-17; secretary of war, September, 1814 to March, 1815; fifth president, 1817-25; chairman, Virginia constitutional convention, 1829.* **Died:** *July 4, 1831, New York City; reinterred, Richmond, Virginia, 1858.*

When news of the Declaration of Independence reached Williamsburg, Virginia, James Monroe left the College of William and Mary to join General Washington's army in New York. Six months later, a tall rawboned lad of 18, Lieutenant Monroe led his men in Washington's crossing of the half-frozen Delaware on Christmas night, 1776. He was in the thick of the surprise attack that routed the Hessians at Trenton, New Jersey. He fought in the hard battles that followed at Brandywine, Germantown, and Monmouth. A bullet he received at Trenton remained in his shoulder for the rest of his life.

After the Revolution, having studied law with his good friend Jefferson, Monroe entered Virginia politics, then served in Congress. During the debates on the Constitution, he opposed its ratification because the charter did not then include a bill of rights and because he felt it gave too much authority to the federal government. In 1794, President Washington appointed him minister to France. "I really thought I was the last man to whom the proposition would be made," Monroe observed. An ardent supporter of the French Revolution, he was highly popular in France. Shortly after the Reign of Terror, Monroe managed to secure the release from prison of both Tom Paine and Mme. de Lafayette.

At home, his mission was not considered successful. Recalled to the United States in 1796, Monroe published a 500-page defense of his conduct in France, with a criticism of Washington's foreign policy. Cool to his former lieutenant, Washington commented: "The truth is, Mr. Monroe was cajoled, flattered, and made to believe strange things. In return, he did or was disposed to do, whatever was pleasing to that nation, reluctantly urging the rights of his own."

Though he had lost Washington's favor, Monroe was twice elected governor of Virginia. In 1803 President Jefferson sent him as minister on new special missions to France, Spain, and England. In France, acting on Jefferson's advice but with great liberty of action, Monroe negotiated with Napoleon the sale of the Louisiana Territory. Monroe always regarded it as his most important public service.

In his mission to Spain, he was unable to reach any agreement regarding Florida, then owned by Spain. In England, after long negotiations with a hostile government, he obtained a treaty which afforded no redress for the capture of American vessels by British cruisers, or for the impressment of American seamen. Refusing to ratify the treaty, Jefferson repudiated Monroe's arrangements. Thus, in less than 10 years, Monroe as minister was disowned by two presidents, Washington and Jefferson.

Ill-paid, impoverished, unable to meet his expenses from his salary, Monroe was ready to retire from public life. In 1811, at the age of 53, he was re-elected

23

governor of Virginia. The same year, President Madison appointed him secretary of state, and, three years later, secretary of war.

During the War of 1812, Monroe proved himself vigorous and effective. When the British raided the capital, he did not hesitate to threaten with the bayonet citizens who urged capitulating to the enemy. He wanted to raise the army to 100,000 men, an unpopular measure. He sent Andrew Jackson to defend the Southwest: "Hasten your militia to New Orleans. Do not wait for this government to arm them. Put all the arms you can into their hands; let every man bring his rifle with him. We shall see you paid."

Elected president in 1816, he was re-elected in 1820 by the remarkable electoral vote of 231 to 1. The single vote against him was cast by a New Hampshire delegate in favor of John Quincy Adams, so that only Washington might have the honor of unanimous election. During his second administration, Monroe secured peaceful boundaries with Canada, obtained Florida from Spain, and supported the anti-slavery position which led to the Missouri Compromise. Earlier, he had aided the settlement of free Negroes in Africa. Monrovia, capital of the first Negro republic, Liberia, was named after him.

His best-known achievement was the Monroe Doctrine, which became a keystone of American foreign policy for more than a century. Monroe proclaimed it in his presidential message of December 2, 1823. Intended to curb the expansionist plans of Russia and Spain, the new policy served warning to European powers that the United States would consider it a threat to her security if any of them attempted fresh colonization on the American continents or if they interfered with existing governments in the western hemisphere. The last referred to the newly independent countries in Central and South America which had revolted against Spain. The Doctrine also indicated that the United States had no designs on Europe and would not interfere in Europe's political affairs. In effect, the Doctrine served as America's second declaration of independence: independence from European power politics.

Six years after he left the White House, Monroe died in his son-in-law's home in New York, on July 4, 1831. Last of the "Virginia dynasty," a faithful servant of the people for 50 years, he was described by Jefferson as a man "whose soul might be turned wrong side outwards without discovering a blemish to the world."

*The tomb of James Monroe at Richmond, Virginia. His remains were brought here from New York City in 1858.*

# John Quincy Adams

**Born:** *July 11, 1767, Braintree (now Quincy), Massachusetts.* **Parents:** *John and Abigail Smith Adams.* **Education:** *Harvard, 1787.* **Married:** *1797, Louisa Catherine Johnson (1775-1852), four children.* **Career:** *lawyer; minister to the Netherlands, 1794-97; minister to Portugal, 1796; minister to Prussia, 1797-1801; member, Massachusetts senate, 1802-03; U.S. senator, 1805-08; professor of rhetoric and belles lettres, Harvard, 1806-09; minister to Russia, 1809-14; minister to Great Britain, 1815-17; secretary of state, 1817-25; sixth president, 1825-29; U.S. representative, 1831-48.* **Died:** *February 23, 1848, Washington, D.C.; buried, Quincy, Mass.*

"I have neither talent nor inclination for intrigue," he remarked when urged to become secretary of state. Though unwilling to play the politician, the boy who had witnessed the Battle of Bunker Hill had held more distinguished offices than any other American. The last man to win the nation's highest office without a party, without courting popularity, without abandoning his lifelong dialogue with his own stern Puritan conscience, he was misunderstood or maligned by most of his contemporaries. His exit from the scene marked the end of a heroic age in the history of the republic. "Mr. Adams is a man of great powers," wrote Emerson, "but chiefly he is a sincere man and not a man of the moment . . . there remains to him the respect of all men for his earnestness."

As a boy of seven, John Quincy Adams witnessed the Battle of Bunker Hill from a rise of land on the family farm at Braintree, Massachusetts. At 10, he accompanied his father on a mission across the blockaded Atlantic and made a three-month trip to Paris by muleback when they were shipwrecked on the Spanish coast. At 14, he became private secretary to the American envoy to Russia. He studied in a private school in Paris and at the University of Leiden before returning to America in 1785 to complete his education at Harvard with the class of 1787.

In 1794, President Washington appointed him minister to the Netherlands and in 1797, when his father became president, he was appointed to the same post in Berlin. However, in 1801, when the elder Adams was defeated in his bid for a second term, he removed his son from the post in order that Jefferson might not have the satisfaction of doing so himself.

*The birthplace of John Quincy Adams in Quincy, Massachusetts. The house is a typical New England salt-box.*

*The reconstructed White House as it looked during Adams' administration. The south portico was added in 1824.*

His election as president in 1824 was bitterly contested. His opponent was Andrew Jackson, the people's turbulent champion. Jackson had received more popular votes and would have been elected if Henry Clay of Kentucky had not thrown his electoral votes to Adams.

Prior to his election, Adams had been denounced as a renegade by the Federalists and suspected by the Jeffersonian Democrats. While serving as senator from Massachusetts, he had voted for both the Louisiana Purchase and the Embargo Act, which most Federalists opposed as unconstitutional. On one occasion, after voting for an unpopular measure, Adams remarked to a colleague, "This measure will cost you and me our seats, but private interests must not be put in opposition to public good." When his prediction came true and he was forced to resign from the Senate, he said: "Far from regretting any one of those acts for which I have suffered, I would do them over again, were they now to be done, at the hazard of ten times as much slander. . . ."

He returned to his law practice in Boston, where he was regarded as a pariah by the Brahmins of Beacon Hill. His father, in retirement at Braintree, had also known what it meant to be "obnoxious, suspected, and unpopular." John Adams wrote approvingly to a son whose character and career so closely

paralleled his own: "You have too honest a heart, too independent a mind, and too brilliant talents to be sincerely and confidentially trusted by any man who is under the domination of party maxims or party feelings."

President Madison sent John Quincy as minister to Russia; President Monroe appointed him minister to England, then secretary of state. Adams negotiated the important treaty with Spain whereby Florida was peacefully ceded to the United States. He also supported the South American colonies in their efforts to free themselves and achieve self-government. He helped to draft the Monroe Doctrine.

As president, succeeding Monroe, he led a Spartan life. He regularly rose at five, built his own fire, read the Bible, bathed in the Potomac—before anyone in the capital was awake. Though he wore shabby clothes, on one occasion, while taking his morning dip, a thief ran away with them. The President was obliged to ask a passing boy to run up to the White House and ask Mrs. Adams for a suit of clothes.

During his term he drew up a broad program to further the arts and sciences and to improve the education of the people. He wanted to establish a national university, to build "the most complete observatory in the world" in the United States. Though many of his plans were blocked by a hostile and divided Congress, he succeeded in establishing the Smithsonian Institution.

Badly defeated by Jackson in 1828, Adams left the White House and retired to his homestead in Quincy, Massachusetts. A voluminous writer, he devoted himself to historical papers. Two years after his retirement, neighbors ventured to ask the ex-President if he would be willing to represent their district in Congress. Adams said he would willingly serve them in any capacity. He made two conditions: First, that he should not be asked to solicit votes or to promote himself; second, that if he were elected he should be free to pursue an independent course.

When the voters in the Plymouth Rock district elected him by an overwhelming majority, the dour old man was much moved. "No other election or appointment conferred upon me ever gave me so much pleasure," he recorded in his *Diary*. "My election as president of the United States was not half so gratifying to my inmost soul!"

At 63, John Quincy Adams began his longest and stormiest period of activity in Washington.

The dispute over slavery was becoming more violent throughout the country. In Congress, petitions were made to abolish slavery in the District of Columbia. To prevent the publication and discussion of such controversial petitions, pro-slavery politicians in Congress tried to pass a gag rule. This was, in effect, a violation of the freedom to petition.

A life-long abolitionist, Congressman Adams opposed it vehemently. "I hold the resolution to be a direct violation of the Constitution of the United States, the rules of this house, and the rights of my constituents!"

When the gag rule was imposed, Adams started his one-man fight with Congress. Year after year he stood on the floor of the House and delivered harsh and forceful arguments against it, presenting hundreds of new petitions to abolish slavery. Derided by his opponents, censured, attacked as an incendiary, threatened with assassination, the tottering old man stood his ground. His voice cracked with age, he carried on the battle until, eight years later, his efforts bore fruit. The gag rule was revoked in 1844, and even his enemies came to respect "Old Man Eloquent," unyielding champion of the rights of man.

A fighter to the end, Adams was on the floor of Congress in February, 1848, when he suffered a stroke. Carried into the Speaker's chamber, the 80-year-old delegate from Plymouth Rock died two days later, with the words: "Thank the officers of the House. This is the last of earth. I am content."

*The Capitol as it looked in 1825. It was burned by the British in 1814; the reconstruction took until late 1824.*

# Andrew Jackson

**Born:** *March 15, 1767, Waxhaw, New Lancaster County, South Carolina.* **Parents:** *Andrew and Elizabeth Hutchinson Jackson.* **Education:** *common school.* **Married:** *1791, Mrs. Rachel Donelson Robards (1767-1828), no children.* **Career:** *saddler's apprentice; farmer; storekeeper; lawyer; soldier; delegate, Tennessee constitutional convention, 1796; U.S. representative, 1796-97; U.S. senator, 1797-98, 1823-25; judge, Supreme Court of Tennessee, 1798-1804; major general, War of 1812; military governor of Florida territory, 1821; seventh president, 1829-37.* **Died:** *June 8, 1845, the Hermitage, near Nashville, Tennessee.*

In contrast to his predecessors, the seventh president rose to power from the poorest and most turbulent elements of frontier society. This fearless soldier and rough-hewn champion of the common man, chosen by small farmers and mechanics, was the first Democrat to enter the White House.

Jefferson, classically educated and a gentleman, did not approve of Jackson. "Good God," he had exclaimed when Jackson had been under consideration as a possible minister to Russia, "he'd breed you a quarrel before he had been there a month!" Yet Jackson's election to the presidency represented a triumph of Jefferson's political philosophy. A second revolution, it heralded the "democratic leveling" which some of the founding fathers had feared.

Jackson's father, a poverty-stricken immigrant from Ireland, had cleared a few acres and built a log cabin in the Waxhaw settlement in South Carolina. Two years after his arrival in America, the father died, leaving a widow with two small sons. A third son, named Andrew, was born a few days after the father's death. The devoted pioneer mother struggled against great odds to maintain her family. She taught Andrew to read. He was nine when a copy of the *Philadelphia Evening Post* with the Declaration of Independence reached the Waxhaw settlement. He was selected to read the great news in front of the general store to a group of some forty frontiersmen—an honor which later became one of Jackson's proudest boasts.

During the latter part of the Revolution, the South was overrun by regiments of redcoats under Lord Cornwallis. In 1780, dragoons swept down over the Waxhaw settlement. At 13, Andrew Jackson was captured as a rebel scout and flung into prison with his brothers. When a British lieutenant ordered Andrew to clean his muddy boots, the tall thin lad with a shock of red hair and fearless blue eyes refused on the

*A painting of Mrs. Rachel Jackson copied from a miniature that Jackson always wore next to his heart.*

"The Brave Boy of the Waxhaws," a Currier & Ives lithograph showing young Andrew and the angry lieutenant.

grounds that he was a prisoner of war, not a servant. The angry lieutenant slashed at Andrew with his sword, scarring him for life. Held in a jail where he nearly starved to death, he caught smallpox. His two brothers died from the hardships. His mother, to whom Jackson was passionately attached, nursed the sick and wounded prisoners until she caught yellow fever and died. She was buried in an unmarked grave.

After the Revolution, alone in the world, young Jackson worked as a saddler's apprentice. When he was 18, one of his neighbors described him as "the most roaring, rollicking, game-cocking, horse-racing, card-playing, mischievous fellow that ever lived in Salisbury . . ."

He studied law and, at 21, was a frontier lawyer in Nashville, Tennessee, in what was then known as the Western District. A prosecuting attorney at 24, he married Rachel Robards, daughter of a Nashville surveyor, under the impression that her first husband, Captain Lewis Robards, had obtained a divorce. Robards had not. When, two years later, this divorce was obtained, the Jacksons remarried. Defending Rachel's reputation, fiery-tempered Jackson fought a number of pistol duels, including one with John Sevier, governor of Tennessee. Governor Sevier at first had refused the challenge. Jackson inserted a notice in the Knoxville newspaper. "Know ye that I, Andrew Jackson, do pronounce, publish, and declare to the world,

that his excellency, John Sevier, is a base coward and poltroon. He will basely insult, but has not the courage to repair. ANDREW JACKSON." A meeting was soon arranged. Although he was in perpetual hot water, his numerous feuds and duels increased his personal popularity.

In 1796, Jackson helped to draft the constitution of Tennessee, which was about to be admitted to the Union as the sixteenth state. He wanted to name the new state "Great Crooked River." The same year he was sent to Congress as Tennessee's first representative, "a tall, lank, uncouth-looking personage . . . with a queue, tied in an eel skin." In 1797, he was elected U.S. senator.

During the War of 1812 he led 2,500 volunteers, including Sam Houston and Davy Crockett, and defeated the Creek Indians in a bloody battle on the Horseshoe Bend of the Tallapoosa River in Alabama. As major general, in command of the South, he marched against the British in Florida and drove them from their base at Pensacola. In January, 1815, he fought his most celebrated battle, successfully defending the vital seaport of New Orleans from British invasion. The battle lasted only half an hour. The enemy losses were 700 killed, 1,400 wounded, 500 captured. Jackson's losses: 8 killed, 13 wounded.

The victory at New Orleans made Jackson a national hero. In 1818, he crushed the Seminole uprising in Florida; he served as Florida's first governor. In 1824, he ran for the presidency against John Quincy Adams and two other candidates. Jackson won more popular votes than any of the other candidates, but since none of them received a majority of the electoral votes the election was forced into the House of Representatives. There Adams was elected president.

In 1828, Jackson won a substantial victory over Adams, receiving more than two-thirds of the electoral votes. Thousands of western settlers made their way to Washington to witness their hero's inaugural. The muddy streets were jammed with men, women, and children who wanted to catch a glimpse of Old Hickory, symbol of the people's bloodless revolution. The lean old man with a shock of white hair took his oath of office on the east porch of the Capitol.

When he completed his address, a wild rush of people surrounded him, and Jackson's friends had to form a ring around him to prevent him from being crushed. Escaping with difficulty, Jackson mounted his horse and started for the White House, pursued by his admirers. Daniel Webster reported how they poured into the White House after the inauguration, broke bowls of punch and stood on satin chairs with their muddy boots while cheering the people's president.

"To the victor belong the spoils" was the new party cry. In his first year Jackson removed some two thousand old office-holders, hereditary postmasters and collectors of the revenue, and gave the jobs to his followers. He felt that any man with common sense could hold public office in a democracy. He gave the important power of patronage to American political parties.

A high-tempered democratic boss who smoked a corncob pipe, kept his pistols oiled, and punctuated his remarks with "By the Eternal!" President Jackson acted decisively on two major issues of the time. One concerned states' rights versus federal rights and involved the tariff of 1828, a federal tax on manufactured imports which agricultural South Carolina considered a "Tariff of Abomination" and declared unconstitutional, null and void. If the federal government attempted to collect the tax, South Carolina threatened to secede from the Union.

*After Jackson's first inauguration, the crowd that followed him to the White House almost took it apart. Women fainted and furniture and china were destroyed. The mob was finally lured onto the lawn by huge tubs of punch.*

*The Hermitage, home of President Jackson near Nashville. His tomb is situated to the right of the mansion.*

While the storm was brewing, Jackson was invited to a Jefferson's birthday dinner where his vice-president, John C. Calhoun of South Carolina, was the chief spokesman for states' rights. Calhoun maintained that each state had the sovereign right to decide when its agent, the federal government, had exceeded its authority. At the dinner Jackson pointedly made his toast a test of loyalty, "Our Federal Union—it shall and must be preserved!" Calhoun answered this with, "Our Union—*next to our liberty*—the most dear!" From this hour, Jackson and Calhoun, both from South Carolina, were enemies.

Determined to deal firmly with South Carolina, Jackson issued his Nullification Proclamation. "I consider the power to annul a law of the United States, assumed by one State, incompatible with the existence of the Union, contradicted expressly by the letter of the Constitution, unauthorized by its spirit, inconsistent with every principle on which it was founded and destructive of the great object for which it was formed."

Old Hickory sent a naval force under David Farragut to Charleston. He ordered General Winfield Scott to ready his troops for a march into South Carolina. He warned the nullifiers that, if a drop of blood were shed, he would hang the first nullifier on the first tree he could find. South Carolina backed down, and the threat of secession was averted.

The second big issue concerned the Bank of the United States.

Headed by Nicholas Biddle, the richest man of the day and an aggressive lobbyist, the Bank had become a financial monopoly which dominated the country's economic life. Jackson was determined to break its power. Against the most vehement opposition (which included Webster, Clay, and Calhoun), he refused to re-charter the Bank. He vetoed bills which had that object. He removed the huge federal deposits of gold from the Bank and distributed them among small new state banks throughout the country. When delegations of New York businessmen complained to Jackson, he told them, "Go to Biddle! We have no money here. Biddle has all the money. . . ." He also declared, *"Andrew Jackson* will never restore the deposits to the Bank! *Andrew Jackson* will never re-charter that monster of corruption!" Sooner than live in a country where such tyrannical power prevailed, he would seek asylum in the wilds of Arabia!

Re-elected in 1832 by an electoral vote of 219 to 49 for Clay, Jackson continued his vigorous fight as the people's champion against the forces of corruption and oppression. Toward the end of his second term he told Van Buren, "When I review the arduous administration through which I have passed, the formidable opposition to its very close of the . . . monied monopolies of the whole country with their corrupting influence with which we had to contend, I am truly thankful to my God for this happy result. . . . It displays the virtue and power of the sovereign people."

Under Jackson's guidance the republic took a giant step toward becoming a democracy. When he retired to the Hermitage, the house he had built near Nashville, Tennessee, his home became a place of pilgrimage for thousands. "Surely he was a great man," observed Nathaniel Hawthorne, "and his native strength, as well of intellect as of character, compelled every man to be his tool that came within his reach; and the more cunning the individual might be, it served only to make him the sharper tool."

31

# Martin Van Buren

**Born:** *December 5, 1782, Kinderhook, New York.*
**Parents:** *Abraham and Mary Hoes Van Buren.*
**Education:** *common school.* **Married:** *1807, Hannah Hoes (1783-1819), four children.* **Career:** *lawyer; surrogate, Columbia County, New York, 1808-13; state senator, 1813-20; attorney general of New York, 1815-19; U.S. senator, 1821-28; governor of New York, January to March, 1829; secretary of state, 1829-31; minister to Great Britain, August, 1831 to January, 1832; vice-president, 1833-37; eighth president, 1837-41.*
**Died:** *July 24, 1862, Kinderhook, New York.*

Groomed by Old Hickory to succeed him, Van Buren kept his promise "to tread generally in the footsteps of President Jackson." Unfortunately, he did not have his predecessor's ability to unite diverse factions through the power of personal appeal. A genial and dapper party boss, he was a virtuoso in the art of double-talk and a wizard in manipulating political strings to advance his own career. Entering the White House in 1837, he ushered in a succession of minor presidents who, for the most part, were unable or unwilling to cope with the issues which finally, when Lincoln was inaugurated in 1861, erupted in the Civil War.

Born of Dutch ancestry in the village of Kinderhook, on a highway between Albany and New York City, Martin Van Buren was the son of a tavern keeper and revealed his political abilities at an early age. Though he never went to college, he studied closely the legislators who made his father's inn a stopping-place to and from Albany. At 14, "Little Van" entered the law office of Francis Sylvester in Kinderhook. At 16, he won his first case as a special pleader in the constable's court where he had to stand on a bench in order to be seen by the jury he addressed. At 18, he was elected to a political nominating convention.

Leaving Kinderhook at the age of 20, Van Buren went to New York City, where he studied to pass his bar examinations. Van Buren developed "extreme caution in avoiding personal collisions," according to John Quincy Adams, and polished his natural charm and affability into a remarkable skill for conciliation. At 30, he was state senator; at 32, attorney general of New York. He welded the first Democratic political machine in New York. It became known as the "Albany Regency," and Van Buren reigned as its undisputed boss.

*Angelica Singleton Van Buren, the wife of Van Buren's oldest son. She was the President's official hostess.*

POLITICAL RACE COURSE - UNION TRACK - FALL RACES 1836

Nº 1 Old Tippecanoe . Nº 2, The Kinderhook Poney . Nº 3, Tennessee White .
Nº 4 Black Dan of Massachusetts

*A typical political cartoon. The contestants are W. H. Harrison, Van Buren, Hugh L. White, and Daniel Webster.*

Elected to the U.S. Senate in 1820, he served there until 1828, when he resigned to lead the campaign for Jackson's presidency. He was credited by his rival, Daniel Webster, with doing more than 10 other men to win it. In the same year Van Buren was elected governor of New York but resigned after two months to become Jackson's secretary of state. Always tactful and adroit, he cemented his friendship with President Jackson in 1830 at the expense of John C. Calhoun, the vice-president. Calhoun's wife had refused to receive Peggy Eaton, wife of the secretary of war, and other cabinet ladies did likewise. The scandalous reason: Peggy, a barmaid in her earlier days, was said to have been Eaton's mistress before their marriage and to have driven her first husband to suicide.

Incensed by the gossip, Jackson declared that Mrs. Eaton was "chaste as a virgin" and made her acceptance a test of loyalty to his administration. Van Buren, a widower since 1819, passed the test by being publicly cordial to her. In 1831, Van Buren resigned as secretary of state. This led to a complete reorganiza-

tion of the cabinet and enabled Jackson to eliminate the supporters of Calhoun.

Van Buren was appointed minister to Great Britian. A year later he was recalled because the Senate refused to ratify his appointment. The deciding vote was cast by Calhoun. "This will kill him," Calhoun gloated; "it will kill him dead." In 1832, however, under Jackson's powerful influence, Van Buren was elected vice-president. In 1836, he was elected president of the United States, defeating William Henry Harrison by an electoral vote of 170 to 73.

He had been in office for only two months when the panic of 1837 swept the country, causing a severe economic depression. It was the second of five in the 19th century, occurring in a "boom-and-bust" cycle in 1819, 1837, 1857, 1873, and 1893. It was caused largely by irresponsible practices in the stock market and by the instability of the banking system which Jackson had attacked in an effort to break the financial monopoly. Unable to meet the spreading demand for payment in gold or silver, the banks (which had been

# A HARD ROAD TO HOE!

*In this cartoon Van Buren is shown weighed down by his plan to establish sub-treasuries throughout the country.*

issuing paper money) closed one after another. Farmers could not sell their crops; mill towns were shut down; the unemployed rioted in New York. Men stood in line for bread or fought for jobs which offered four dollars a month in wages.

Though besieged by embittered voters and though he knew his course would lose him the next election, Van Buren held to his policy of not interfering with the economic life of the country. A Jeffersonian democrat, as well as a disciple of Jackson, he believed that government best which governed least. "All communities are apt to look to government for too much, especially at periods of sudden embarrassment or distress . . ." he said. "Those who look to this government for specific aid lose sight of the ends for which it was created, and the powers with which it is clothed. . . . It was not intended to confer special favors on individuals or on any classes of them . . ."

As a remedy to financial panic, Van Buren proposed that government deposits of gold be locked in an independent treasury, with sub-treasuries in key areas. He fought for the measure for four years; it was passed by Congress, then repealed, then re-introduced. The banking system remained substantially the same until Woodrow Wilson's Federal Reserve Act of 1913 stabilized it. Not until Franklin Roose-

velt's New Deal program of 1933 did the federal government take steps to deal directly with economic crises.

Though increasingly unpopular, President Van Buren—with his fringes of white hair and mutton-chop whiskers—remained an imperturbable old dandy. The poor innkeeper's son from Kinderhook had become a Beau Brummel who perfumed his whiskers, loved champagne, ate his meals from gold plate, and laced himself tightly in corsets. Extravagantly abused and caricatured, nicknamed "The Machiavellian Belshazzar," he was re-nominated in 1840 but went down to the tunes of "Van! Van! Is a used-up man!" and "Tippecanoe and Tyler, Too!" Harrison won with a 4 to 1 majority.

In 1844 Van Buren lost his party's nomination to Polk because he would not endorse the annexation of Texas. He broke with the Democratic party in 1848 to become the candidate of the anti-slavery Free Soil party, whose slogan was "Free soil, free speech, free labor, and free men!" Although he did not receive a single electoral vote, his candidacy split the Democratic vote and helped elect General Zachary Taylor, hero of the Mexican War. Surviving his presidency by 20 years, Van Buren died at Lindenwald, his estate at Kinderhook, in 1862, at the age of 79.

# William Henry Harrison

**Born:** *February 9, 1773, Berkeley, Charles City County, Virginia.* **Parents:** *Benjamin and Elizabeth Bassett Harrison.* **Education:** *Hampden-Sydney College, 1787-1790.* **Married:** *1795, Anna Symmes (1775-1864), ten children.* **Career:** *farmer; U.S. Army, 1791-98, 1812-14; secretary, Northwest Territory, 1798-99; territorial delegate to Congress, 1799-1801; governor, Territory of Indiana, 1801-12; U.S. representative from Ohio, 1816-19; member, Ohio senate, 1819-21; U.S. senator, 1825-28; minister to Colombia, 1828-29; county clerk, 1834-40; ninth president, March 4 to April 4, 1841.* **Died:** *April 4, 1841, Washington, D.C.; buried, North Bend, Ohio.*

The first American to be ballyhooed into the highest office, the last president who was born a British subject, at 68 Harrison was the oldest president to enter the White House. He was the first to die in it, after the shortest tenure: one month in office. Though the frenzied campaign before his election featured him as a western folk hero of "log cabin and cider" fame, Harrison was born a Virginia aristocrat, his "cabin" had 22 rooms, and he had run a whisky distillery on his Ohio farm.

Third son of Benjamin Harrison, who was a signer of the Declaration and a close friend of George Washington, the future president was born on the family plantation in Berkeley, Virginia. After attending Hampden-Sidney College, he entered the University of Pennsylvania at 18 to study medicine. Four months later he left school to become a soldier. Commissioned by President Washington, he served under General Anthony Wayne at Fallen Timbers in the Indian War of 1794, was mentioned for gallantry and promoted to captain. In 1795 he married Anna Symmes, daughter of a prominent Territorial judge. In 19 years she bore him 10 children.

Resigning his commission in 1798, Harrison was appointed secretary of the Northwest Territory, by President John Adams. Threatened by frequent Indian raids, the Territory was a frontier region bounded by the Great Lakes on the north, the Ohio River on the south and the Mississippi on the west. Harrison held the post for 12 years, becoming Superintendent of Indian Affairs, then governor of the Territory under Presidents Jefferson and Madison.

Considered capable, just, and patient, Harrison negotiated treaties with Indian tribes and bought large tracts of land from them for the government. One parcel included three million acres on the Wabash and White Rivers. Discouraging speculators, he divided the public lands into small tracts for the benefit of poor settlers. He tried to improve the Indians' condition, urging them to become farmers, prohibiting the sale of liquor among them, inoculating them against the smallpox.

But the Indian tribes were becoming increasingly hostile; within 14 years they had lost hunting grounds which amounted to 48 million acres. The great Shawnee chief, Tecumseh, started to unite the tribes and to crusade against the settlers, with his brother, who was known as "The Prophet." They led the Creeks, Choctaws, and Cherokees in bloody frontier raids. Harrison held parleys with Tecumseh but failed to pacify the chief. In November, 1811, Harrison called for volunteers from the Territory; he marched with 800 men to Tippecanoe, in Indiana. On November 7, before dawn, the Indians struck. General Harrison responded with a fierce cavalry charge which toppled the Indians and killed their leader, "The Prophet."

In the second year of the War of 1812, Harrison was commissioned major general, in charge of all troops in the Northwest. Following Peary's victory on Lake Erie, he entered Canada with his troops. On October 5, 1813, he defeated the British forces and their Indian allies. Tecumseh was killed in the battle, and the Great Lakes were saved for the United States. Harrison became a national hero.

The next year, because of a slight he received from the secretary of war, Harrison resigned from the army. Between 1816 and 1828 he served terms in Congress and the Senate. In 1828, he was appointed minister to Colombia by President John Quincy Adams. While in Bogotá he wrote to Simon Bolívar, the liberator of South America, and exhorted him against becoming a dictator. "To be eminently great it is necessary to be eminently good," wrote Harrison in a letter which was considered a breach in diplomatic etiquette. In 1829, he was recalled from South America by President Andrew Jackson.

Retiring to his farm at North Bend, Ohio, the lean old Indian fighter spent the next dozen years in obscurity, deep in debt, with many dependents, and unable to get a new appointment. John Quincy Adams described him as "a political adventurer . . . whose thirst for lucrative office is absolutely rabid." In 1834, at the age of 61, Harrison became clerk of the Hamilton County Court. From that minor post he reached the presidency in a single step.

In 1840, the newly formed Whig party was looking for a vote-getter whose opinions were unknown. The Whigs rejected the natural contenders, Henry Clay and Daniel Webster, as having too many enemies. They settled on Harrison, with John Tyler of Virginia as his running mate to bring in the southern vote. According to Senator Thomas Hart Benton, "the only ability sought by the Whigs was availability." Before his nomination, financier Nicholas Biddle advised that Harrison "say not one single word about his principles. Let him say nothing. . . . Let the use of pen and ink be wholly forbidden to him."

Launching the noisiest election campaign in American history, the Whigs organized mammoth rallies, torchlight processions, parades and floats with cider casks and log cabins on wheels. They pushed a giant ball of paper inscribed with the slogan "Keep the ball rolling" to Washington. They shouted themselves hoarse with campaign songs and the battle cry "Tippecanoe and Tyler, Too!" Amid circus-like ballyhoo Harrison won by a landslide, at the expense of the "monarchist," Martin Van Buren. "We have been sung down, lied down, drunk down," complained the Democrats. "Harrison comes in upon a hurricane," observed Adams. "God grant he may not go out upon a wreck."

On the cold and rainy day of his inaugural, the 68-year-old "Washington of the West" refused to wear an overcoat. To show he was in good health he rode on horseback in a parade for two hours. He took his oath of office bareheaded and delivered the longest inaugural speech on record, a speech which Daniel Webster had vainly tried to edit. Over-exposed, Harrison caught a cold which developed into pneumonia. He died on April 4, 1841, exactly one month after his inaugural, the first president to die in office.

*Harrison is shown in the left foreground in this lithograph of the Battle of the Thames, October 5, 1813.*

# John Tyler

**Born:** *March 29, 1790, Greenway, Charles City County, Virginia.* **Parents:** *John and Mary Armistead Tyler.* **Education:** *William and Mary, 1807.* **Married:** *1813, Letitia Christian (1790-1842), eight children; 1844, Julia Gardiner (1820-89), seven children.* **Career:** *lawyer; member, Virginia house of delegates, 1811-16, 1823-25, 1839-41; U.S. representative, 1816-21; governor of Virginia, 1825-27; U.S. senator, 1827-36; member, Virginia constitutional convention, 1829, 1830; vice-president, March 4 to April 6, 1841; tenth president, 1841-45.* **Died:** *January 18, 1862, Richmond, Virginia.*

Born in Charles City County in Virginia, John Tyler was the second son of Judge John Tyler, a good personal friend of Jefferson. A mild and tractable boy, he was fond of music and poetry and a fair performer on the violin. At the age of 11, young Tyler was ringleader in a revolt against a bullying schoolmaster, William McMurdo. Too fond of applying the birch, McMurdo was overpowered by his pupils one day, tied hand and foot, trussed, and locked up in the schoolhouse. Later, when the indignant schoolmaster complained, Judge Tyler's comment was, *"Sic semper tyrannis."*

Graduating from the College of William and Mary in 1807, John Tyler was admitted to the bar, then entered Virginia politics. An honest but undistinguished legislator, in the course of the next 30 years he served as governor of Virginia and in the U.S. Senate. At 23, he had married Letitia Christian, daughter of a planter; she died in the White House in 1842. In the last year of his term, Tyler, aged 54, married 24-year-old Julia Gardiner of New York, a May-December union which added to his unpopularity. Tyler fathered more children than any other president—15—eight by Letitia Christian and seven by Julia Gardiner.

On the national scene he was called "Turncoat Tyler" for first supporting then opposing Andrew Jackson and for being a Southern Whig in 1835, a Whig in 1840, a Democrat in 1844. When Tyler became president, Jackson announced from his retreat at the Hermitage that the country now had "an imbecile in the Executive Chair, a mere puppet. . . ."

Although the Constitution did not grant full powers to the vice-president who succeeded to the presidency due to the death of his predecessor, John Tyler—the first vice-president to so succeed—took the full powers and set enduring precedents.

Soon after Tyler became president, Daniel Webster rose in the cabinet and told him that it had been Harrison's custom to accept the vote of the majority in his cabinet on all administrative measures and to limit himself to a single simple vote. The strong men in the cabinet intended to dominate Tyler. But in the suave Virginia gentleman they had caught a tiger by the tail.

"I am president," Tyler informed them, "and I shall be held responsible for my administration. I hope I shall have your hearty cooperation. So long as you see fit to do this, I shall be glad to have you with me. When you think otherwise, I shall be equally glad to receive your resignation."

Tyler repeatedly exercised his veto power to defeat such measures as Clay's bill to set up a new Bank of the United States. He vetoed high-tariff bills. A states' rights advocate, he fought Clay over improvements within the states at government expense. Tyler was disowned and denounced by the Whigs, burnt in effigy on the White House lawn, threatened with impeachment and assassination. Within six months of his inaugural, his entire cabinet resigned with the exception of Webster, who wanted to finish a treaty with the British which he had begun. When Webster finished it, he resigned, too.

In February of 1844 Tyler narrowly escaped death in a tragic accident aboard the new propeller-driven battleship, *Princeton*. The president was entertaining several hundred guests on a sail down the Potomac. To demonstrate the ship's 12-inch gun the crew fired a salvo. The cannon exploded and burst at the breech. Tyler was below decks at the time and out of danger, but several diplomats, naval officers and cabinet members were killed or injured in the blast. Among the dead was the new secretary of state, Abel Upshur.

Tyler replaced him with John C. Calhoun. This served to shift the balance of power to the South. Opposed to the growing might of Northern industrial tycoons and the voting power in the hands of city mobs, Tyler consistently furthered the interests of the "Southern Republic" which Calhoun envisioned as an agrarian society ruled by an educated aristocracy.

During the latter half of Tyler's administration, the proposed annexation of Texas became a hotly debated issue. Texas wanted to be part of the Union, but the admission of Texas as a slave state would shatter the existing balance between slave and free states, between the North and the South. John Quincy Adams said that the annexation of Texas was "so injurious as not only inevitably to result in a dissolution of the Union, but fully to justify it." Tyler fought for the treaty of annexation. After being rejected by the Senate, it was finally passed in a joint resolution by both Houses of Congress largely through the efforts of Calhoun, then secretary of state. On March 3, 1845, his last day in office, Tyler signed the measure which admitted Texas into the Union.

Tyler retired to his estate in Virginia and remained in obscurity for the next 16 years. For a time he was employed as county road supervisor. Meanwhile, the great and bitter tension between the North and the South was approaching the breaking point. In 1861, Tyler re-appeared briefly in Washington as head of a peace committee from the South. When their proposals were ignored, Tyler declared that there was nothing left for Virginia but to exercise her rights as a sovereign state and secede from the Union.

Elected to the Confederate House of Representatives, in revolt against the United States, Tyler did not live to see the congress convene. He died on January 18, 1862, in Richmond, at the age of 72. He was considered a rebel by the government he once headed, and no official announcement of his death was made.

*The two wives of President Tyler: left, Letitia Christian; right, Julia Gardiner. He had 15 children by them.*

# James K. Polk

**Born:** *November 2, 1795, Mecklenburg County, North Carolina.* **Parents:** *Samuel and Jane Knox Polk.* **Education:** *University of North Carolina, 1818.* **Married:** *1824, Sarah Childress (1803-91), no children.* **Career:** *store clerk; lawyer; member, Tennessee legislature, 1823-25; U.S. representative, 1825-39; speaker of the House, 1835-39; governor of Tennessee, 1839-41; eleventh president, 1845-49.* **Died:** *June 15, 1849, Nashville, Tennessee.*

Of 11 presidents, James Knox Polk was the eighth Southerner to be elected. Born in Mecklenburg County, North Carolina, he was raised on his father's farm in Duck River Valley in frontier Tennessee. His ancestors were Scotch-Irish immigrants who spelled their name Pollok. His mother was a great grand-niece of the religious reformer, John Knox. A thin, frail, sickly boy, rather shy and secretive, he learned mathematics while accompanying his father on surveying trips. An industrious student, he graduated from the University of North Carolina in 1818 with top honors in mathematics and the classics.

Entering the law office of a political leader in Nashville, he met Andrew Jackson shortly before Jackson's appointment as military governor of Florida. As a campaigner in local politics and a witty and sarcastic orator, Polk was nicknamed "Napoleon of the Stumps." At 28, he was a member of the Tennessee house of representatives and secured passage of a bill against dueling. Next year he was sent to Congress where he served seven terms. At 40, he was Speaker of the House; at 44, governor of Tennessee. In 1844, he was nominated for the presidency.

"The least conspicuous man who had ever been nominated for president," Polk was the first dark horse to win the race. He became one of the most successful chief executives. A perfect party man, a friend and disciple of Jackson, he had drawn up his program before he entered the White House. He carried out his program in a single term, then quit the scene altogether, having added more territory to the United States than anyone since Jefferson made the Louisiana Purchase.

At the Democratic Convention in Baltimore in 1844 the most controversial issue was the annexation of Texas. Martin Van Buren, the party leader, opposed it on anti-slavery grounds. Henry Clay of Kentucky, the Whig candidate and "Great Compromiser,"

*Mrs. James K. Polk. With her dark eyes and olive complexion, she was considered very handsome.*

*The White House as it looked during Polk's administration. By 1848 the mansion looked much as it does today.*

quibbled and qualified until he alienated the abolitionists and compromised his last chance for the highest office. When Polk was asked his opinion, he said: "I have no hesitation in declaring that I am in favor of immediate re-annexation of Texas to the government and territory of the United States."

These bold words expressed the hopes of the majority. The term "re-annexation" was artful. It was based on an early claim which held that Texas was part of the Louisiana Purchase. The claim had been ceded to Spain by John Quincy Adams in 1819. Since then, however, Mexico had declared her independence from Spain, and Texas had declared her independence from Mexico. The Republic of Texas wanted to be admitted to the Union. Polk's views were in tune with the visions of the expansionists concerning America's "manifest destiny" and with the ever-increasing westward migration of people across the continent. The expansion toward the Pacific Ocean, through the Southwest, threatened to lead to a war with Mexico. The expansion through the Northwest and the Oregon Territory threatened a war with Great Britain.

At the start of his term Polk stated the four objectives of his administration: the reduction of the tariff, the re-establishment of the independent treasury, the acquisition of California, and the settlement of the Oregon boundary question with Great Britain. A cold, austere, seemingly colorless magistrate, he worked diligently and attained all four of his objectives.

American claims in the Northwest extended as far north as Alaska, while the British claim ran down as far as Portland, Oregon, and the Columbia River. Though he never intended to fight for all of the American claim, Polk let his campaigners shout themselves

hoarse with the slogan "Fifty-four forty, or fight!" This referred to the parallel of latitude which would satisfy the United States as the boundary between herself and Canada. In office, he arranged a compromise with Great Britain which set the boundary at the forty-ninth parallel.

The annexation of Texas (which President Tyler had signed at the end of his term) was followed by disputes over boundaries in the Southwest. Texas claimed the Rio Grande as the boundary; Mexico claimed the Nueces River, 200 miles north of the Rio Grande. A skirmish in the disputed area gave President Polk an excuse to declare war against Mexico. "Mexico has invaded our territory," he solemnly told Congress in May, 1846, "and shed American blood upon American soil." The Mexican War was considered imperialistic by part of Congress. One representative, 37-year-old Abraham Lincoln of Illinois, demanded to know upon what exact spot on American soil the American blood had been shed. Next year Lincoln voted for a resolution, passed by the House, which thanked the American officers for their services "in a war unnecessarily and unconstitutionally begun by the President of the United States." Another American who disapproved of the Mexican War, Henry David Thoreau, refused to pay his poll-tax of one dollar because the money might be used "to buy a man or a musket to shoot one with." Thoreau was put in the Concord jail, an event which later led to the writing of his essay on "Civil Disobedience."

The Mexican War made a national hero out of General Zachary Taylor, "Old Rough and Ready," who defeated Santa Anna at Buena Vista. It raised the presidential aspirations of General Winfield Scott,

"Fuss and Feathers," who captured Mexico City in 1847, and whose army included two young West Point graduates, Robert E. Lee and U. S. Grant. By a treaty of peace signed in February, 1848, Mexico ceded the New Mexico Territory and California—522,568 square miles—for $15 million.

Polk left the White House in March, 1849. Three months later he was dead, a victim of illness and overwork. At the age of 53, he met the youngest death of any presidents except Garfield and Kennedy, who were assassinated. Historian George Bancroft, judging Polk by the results of his administration, considered him "one of the very best, most honest and most successful presidents the country ever had."

*A contemporary artist's view of Polk's inauguration. It was said that he spoke "to a large assemblage of umbrellas."*

In four decades of fighting, Taylor never lost a battle. A completely fearless man, he detested war. "I sincerely rejoice at the prospect of peace," he once wrote. "My life has been devoted to arms, yet I look upon war at all times, and under all circumstances, as a national calamity, to be avoided if compatible with the national honor."

He was born in Orange County, Virginia, but was still in swaddling clothes when his family moved to Kentucky and the log cabin in which, mostly unschooled, he grew to manhood. More than from books, his education took shape from the talk of battles and warfare that he heard around his home. His father, Richard Taylor, had been a colonel and a hero in the Revolutionary War. It was not surprising, therefore, that at 23 Zachary Taylor joined the army as a lieutenant.

*An 1848 lithograph of General Taylor's great victory at Buena Vista, which made him a national hero.*

"A LITTLE MO[

# Zachary Taylor

**Born:** *November 24, 1784, Montebello, Orange County, Virginia.* **Parents:** *Richard and Sarah Strother Taylor.* **Education:** *common school.* **Married:** *1810, Margaret Smith (1788-1852), six children.* **Career:** *U.S. Army, 1808-49; twelfth president, March 5, 1849 to July 9, 1850.* **Died:** *July 9, 1850, Washington, D.C.; buried, Louisville, Kentucky.*

Although other presidents had taken up arms in the service of their country, Zachary Taylor was the first career soldier to rise to the nation's highest office without having held any other civil post, either by election or by appointment. He and William Henry Harrison were the only two presidents the Whig party ever elected. Both men were national heroes—and both died in office.

During the War of 1812, Taylor commanded a tiny garrison of fifty sick and disabled soldiers at Fort Harrison in Indiana. Besieged by Indian forces under Tecumseh, he was outnumbered ten to one. Rallying his men, Taylor repulsed the final attack in a desperate, hand-to-hand battle.

For the next forty years he knew no other life than that of a soldier. He took little interest in politics and never even voted till he was 62. But politics took an interest in him.

The Mexican War had made him a national hero. At the head of 5,000 American volunteers, "Old Rough and Ready" had defeated Santa Anna and a force nearly four times the size of his own in the battle of Buena Vista.

At the height of the battle, his officers pleaded with him to retire to safer ground, out of the enemy's range of fire. "Let us ride nearer," he answered, "and then their balls will go over us."

Taylor was no picture-book soldier. He was a squat

little man who had to be boosted into his saddle. He hated military pomp and ceremony so much that he seldom wore a uniform, preferring to fight in the simple clothes that he wore on his Louisiana farm.

The victory at Buena Vista thrust Taylor into national prominence near the end of Polk's single term in office. Although his political views were unknown to them, the Whigs picked Taylor at their nominating convention of 1848. The nomination was mailed to him, but because it came with 10¢ postage due, Taylor, not knowing what it was, sent it back. The party and its candidate soon got together and a noisy campaign, similar to the circus-like one of 1840 for Harrison, was staged on his behalf.

"Old Rough and Ready" won the election by a popular vote of 1,370,101 to 1,220,544 for Lewis Cass, the Democratic candidate. In March, 1849, at age 64, he was inaugurated. Though he himself was a Southerner and a slaveholder, and four out of his seven cabinet members were Southerners, Taylor proved steadfast in his loyalty to the Union. He approved California's admission as a free state and recommended the same course for New Mexico. To threats of secession from the South he replied that he was ready and willing to take his place at the head of the army to preserve the Union. He promised "to hang any man taken in treason."

In his message to Congress in 1849, Taylor urged the cessation of sectional disputes. He was largely ignored by a Congress which was dominated by Daniel Webster, Henry Clay, and John C. Calhoun—each of whom had more burning ambitions for the presidency than Taylor. In the heated final debates, Webster recommended concessions to the South for the "preservation of the Union." This resulted in the passage of what became known as Clay's Compromise of 1850. The Compromise provided for the admission of California as a free state, with slavery optional in New Mexico and Utah, and for the abolition of the slave trade, but not of slavery, in the District of Columbia. To please the South, it included a drastic fugitive slave act. Taylor opposed this as an appeasement of the South, but was unable to do much to avert the coming conflict.

On the Fourth of July, 1850, while taking part in ceremonies held at the then-unfinished Washington Monument, Taylor stood long in the broiling sun. Returning to the White House, he drank iced milk and ate handfuls of fresh cherries. Within an hour he was violently ill. "I should not be surprised if this were to terminate in death," said the 65-year-old veteran. "I did not expect to encounter what has beset me since my elevation to the presidency. . . . I have been mistaken, my motives have been misconstrued, my feelings grossly betrayed . . ." Five days later, "Old Rough and Ready" was dead.

# Millard Fillmore

**Born:** *January 7, 1800, Summerhill, Cayuga County, New York.* **Parents:** *Nathaniel and Phoebe Millard Fillmore.* **Education:** *common school.* **Married:** *1826, Abigail Powers (1798-1853), two children; 1858, Mrs. Caroline Carmichael McIntosh (1813-81), no children.* **Career:** *wool carder; teacher; postmaster; lawyer; counsellor, New York Supreme Court, 1829; New York state assembly, 1829-31; U.S. representative, 1833-35, 1837-43; comptroller of New York, 1848-49; vice-president, March 5, 1849 to July 9, 1850; thirteenth president, 1850-53.* **Died:** *March 8, 1874, Buffalo, New York.*

Born on a frontier farm in Cayuga County, Millard Fillmore was raised in New York's Finger Lakes district. Apprenticed to a clothmaker at 15 and resenting his master's harsh treatment, he bought back his freedom for $30 and returned home on foot, walking a distance of some hundred miles. For nine months out of the year he worked on the family farm; for three months he attended a one-room schoolhouse where his teacher was Miss Abigail Powers, a Baptist clergyman's daughter and Fillmore's future wife. Until he was 19 and bought himself a dictionary, Fillmore had no books in his home except the family Bible. He had never seen a copy of Shakespeare nor a map of the United States.

Encouraged by Abigail, he studied law. At 23, a tall husky man who never touched tobacco or liquor, he was admitted to the New York bar. At 26, he married Abigail. At 28, he was elected to the state assembly; at 33, he was in Congress; at 48, Comptroller of New York; at 50, president of the United States. Finding no books in the White House, not even a Bible, Abigail set aside one room for a library and obtained an appropriation of $250 from Congress to buy books for it. She also caused a stir by installing the first bathtub in the White House.

As president Fillmore supported the constitutional argument that slavery should be free to spread wherever it would. He endorsed the Compromise of 1850 and signed the drastic Fugitive Slave Law. In doing so, he put an end to his own political future and signed the death warrant of the Whig party.

During his administration, Fillmore sent Commodore Matthew C. Perry with a fleet to Japan and opened up trade with that distant empire. The Hungarian freedom fighter Louis Kossuth visited the United States, in an effort to gain support for Hungary's fight against Hapsburg domination. He was the guest of honor at a dinner where Daniel Webster, then secretary of state, offered the toast: "Hungarian independence, Hungarian control of her own destinies, and Hungary as a distinct nationality among the nations of Europe." President Fillmore received Kossuth at the White House, but made it clear to him that the United States could not intervene in European conflicts.

He refused a degree from Oxford on the ground that he had neither literary nor scientific attainment. In his last message to Congress, he opposed the idea of securing Cuba as a new state in the Union.

Failing to be re-nominated in 1852, Fillmore made another bid in 1856, becoming the first and last presidential candidate of the Know-Nothing Party. A semi-secret organization, the Know-Nothings were opposed to immigration and they fought against the appointment of Roman Catholics or the foreign-born to government posts. Fillmore carried only one state, Maryland. He then retired to Buffalo, New York, where he took part in educational and philanthropic activities until his death in 1874.

*"Judge Wood Assists Young Fillmore." The young wool carder had the good fortune to meet Judge Walter Wood, who took him into his office to study law. Fillmore stayed with him for two years.*

*Five years after the death of his first wife, Fillmore married Mrs. Caroline Carmichael McIntosh, a wealthy widow. After this marriage, he bought the largest mansion in Buffalo (below) where he lived until his death in 1874.*

# Franklin Pierce

**Born:** *November 23, 1804, Hillsboro, New Hampshire.* **Parents:** *Benjamin and Anna Kendrick Pierce.* **Education:** *Bowdoin College, 1824.* **Married:** *1834, Jane Means Appleton (1806-63), three children.* **Career:** *lawyer; member, New Hampshire legislature, 1829-33; U.S. representative, 1833-37; U.S. senator, 1837-42; brigadier general, Mexican War, 1847-48; fourteenth president, 1853-57.* **Died:** *October 8, 1869, Concord, New Hampshire.*

A brigadier general in the Mexican War, Pierce was a military hero. A graduate of Bowdoin, where his friends and classmates had included Nathaniel Hawthorne and Henry Wadsworth Longfellow, he was a fluent orator, a gay convivial gentleman, handsome as a matinee idol.

A Democrat from New Hampshire, where his father was a Democratic leader, Pierce was the second dark horse, the third New Englander, and the youngest candidate, at 48, to be elected president. Unknown to the country at large, unambitious for political honors, he did not seek the presidency. Though he made no campaign speeches, he defeated pompous General Scott of the dying Whig party by the overwhelming electoral vote of 254 to 42.

Though Pierce himself was fond of gay society, his private life was shadowed by tragedy. His bride had a morbid aversion to social life. On her wishes, Pierce resigned his seat in the U.S. Senate, refused other offices, and retired to Concord, New Hampshire. Two of their three sons died in infancy. Their last child, a boy of 11, died in a railroad wreck between Concord and Boston shortly before the Pierces left for Washington for the inaugural in March, 1853. The parents saw their son killed when their coach rolled down an embankment. Grief-stricken, Mrs. Pierce ascribed the loss of her son to her husband's election. God, she felt, had taken her son so that her husband's mind would be free from any distraction.

Choosing his cabinet, Pierce appointed Jefferson Davis as his secretary of war. An able Southerner, Davis was to become president of the Confederacy less than a decade later. Though Pierce held the mandate of the whole nation, he yielded to the strong pro-slavery pressure groups in the capital. Senator Stephen A. Douglas, a spellbinder with presidential aspirations, persuaded Congress to repeal the Missouri Compromise and offered in its place the Kansas-Nebraska bill. This opened Kansas to settlers who would themselves decide whether or not to admit slavery. In 1854, Pierce forced the bill through Congress by making it a test of loyalty to the Democratic party. As a result, rival legislatures were set up in Kansas. Armed bands crossed over from Missouri to vote for slavery, then return home. Bitter feuds followed, with charges of election fraud. When the "free staters" set up their own government, Congress refused to recognize it. The guerrilla warfare between the pro-slavery and free-state settlers gave the area the name "Bleeding Kansas." A civil war in miniature, the conflict was climaxed by John Brown's bloody raid on Pottawatomie Creek in 1855. The struggle in Kansas remained unresolved during Pierce's single term. It was finally won by the Free-soilers.

During his administration three U.S. ministers who had been negotiating the purchase of Cuba from Spain drew up the Ostend Manifesto. This declared that if Spain refused to sell Cuba, the United States would take Cuba by force. The abolitionists decried the expansionist and pro-slavery manifesto. Pierce ignored it and the negotiations failed. Defeated for re-election in 1856, Pierce retired to Concord, New Hampshire, where he died 13 years later, discarded by his party and forgotten by most of his former friends.

IN UNION IS STRENGTH

THE UNION MUST AND SHALL BE PRESERVED

FOR PRESIDENT          FOR VICE PRESIDENT.

FRANKLIN PIERCE.          WILLIAM R. KING.

THE UNION NOW AND FOREVER.

# James Buchanan

**Born:** *April 23, 1791, Cove Gap, near Mercersburg, Franklin County, Pennsylvania.* **Parents:** *James and Elizabeth Speer Buchanan.* **Education:** *Dickinson College, 1809.* **Married:** *Bachelor.* **Career:** *lawyer; volunteer, War of 1812; member, Pennsylvania legislature, 1815-16; U.S. representative, 1821-31; minister to Russia, 1832-33; U.S. senator, 1834-45; secretary of state, 1845-49; minister to Great Britain, 1853-56; fifteenth president, 1857-61.* **Died:** *June 1, 1868, Wheatland, near Lancaster, Pennsylvania.*

"You are sleeping on a volcano," his attorney general warned him. "Without prompt and energetic action, you will be the last president of the United States." But the new chief executive preferred to remain deaf to Edwin M. Stanton's warning. At 65, James Buchanan was too old, too cautious, too indecisive. A

holder of office for 40 years, he had more experience in government than anyone since John Quincy Adams. Unable to cope with the long-brewing domestic problem which threatened to split the Union, his policy was to watch and wait. Originally a rich, conservative lawyer from Pennsylvania, he was a well-meaning gentleman, a pious Presbyterian of Scotch-Irish origin, fond of social life in the capital.

Son of an immigrant from Ireland, Buchanan was raised on the family farm in Franklin County, Pennsylvania. His father later became a prosperous storekeeper in Mercersburg. A clever student, Buchanan graduated from Dickinson College at the head of his class. Before he was 30 he had earned $300,000 from his legal practice. His prosperity was marred in 1819 when his beautiful bride-to-be broke their engagement, due to a misunderstanding, and died shortly afterwards. Buchanan never married. He served in Congress for 10 years; then, from the age of 43 to 54 in the Senate. President Jackson sent him as minister to Russia; Polk made him secretary of state; Pierce, minister to England. Negotiating with Spain, Buchanan was one of the three ministers who drafted the unfortunate Ostend Manifesto.

The Democratic nomination came to him unsought on his return from England. Though he had been a presidential aspirant for 20 years, the honor had been withheld from him until he was too old to enjoy it. As Buchanan put it, "All the enemies I hated and

*In 1860 the Prince of Wales visited the United States. With the President, he visited the tomb of Washington.*

48

Mr. SHADBLOW, having voted for the successful candidate, resolves to be at the *Inauguration*.

Having reached Washington, he goes to the Hotel and asks for "A Nice Room, not too high up."

The "Gentlemanly Clerk" gives him his choice of the Roof or the Kitchen.—He prefers the latter.

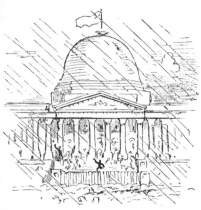

The glorious moment arrives. Mr. Shadblow witnesses the Inauguration—at a distance.

He falls in with a "Member of the House," who introduces him to a "Senator."

Having parted with his Honorable Friends, he finds that he has lost his Pocket-Book.

*From* Harper's Monthly, *April, 1857. Mr. Shadblow concluded that there was great corruption in Washington.*

marked for punishment are turned my friends." His rival in the race of 1856 was John Charles Frémont, the dashing 43-year-old soldier, explorer, and senator from California. Crusading against slavery, Frémont was the choice of the newly formed Republican party, then the party of militant western liberals and New England intellectuals. In the contest between "Old Buck" and "Young America," Buchanan was heavily backed by northern banking and industrial interests who feared the South's threats to secede if the Republicans came into power. Though Buchanan did not get the popular majority, he won the electoral vote, which tallied 174 for Buchanan, 114 for Frémont, and 8 for Millard Fillmore.

At his inaugural on March 4, 1857, President Buchanan asked the country to stand behind an important forthcoming decision of the Supreme Court. Two days later the chief justice, 79-year-old Roger B. Taney, delivered the decision. It concerned the highly controversial case of Dred Scott, an elderly Negro who had been born a slave in Virginia but who had been living on free soil in Missouri for 15 years. To prevent his seizure as a runaway slave, Scott had been appealing his case through the lower courts for

several years. The Supreme Court now turned down his appeal, and Taney, a conservative from Maryland, ruled that all former federal restrictions of slavery were null and void and any effort to legislate against slavery was unconstitutional. A Negro was not a citizen, whether bond or free, and, being property, could not plead his case in court.

The Dred Scott decision raised a violent storm of protest against the Court and the Buchanan administration. It was followed by Abraham Lincoln's debates with Senator Douglas in 1858, which further intensified the issue. In the next year John Brown, the fanatical abolitionist who tried to arm the slaves, was seized at Harpers Ferry and hanged for treason. In 1860, South Carolina seceded, soon followed by six other states. Trying to face both ways, Buchanan said that the slave states had no legal right to secede, but, on the other hand, the federal government had no legal right to put down the states' rebellion.

Damned by both sides, Buchanan left the White House in 1861. He retired to his estate in Lancaster, Pennsylvania. Having survived the administrations of sixteen presidents, from George Washington to Abraham Lincoln, he died in 1868 at the age of 77.

# Abraham Lincoln

**Born:** *February 12, 1809, near Hodgenville, Hardin (now Larue) County, Kentucky.* **Parents:** *Thomas and Nancy Hanks Lincoln.* **Education:** *common school.* **Married:** *1842, Mary Todd (1818-82), four children.* **Career:** *farm hand; store clerk; surveyor; postmaster; lawyer; member, Illinois legislature, 1835-43; U.S. representative, 1847-49; sixteenth president, 1861-65.* **Died:** *April 15, 1865, Washington, D.C.; buried, Springfield, Illinois.*

Abraham Lincoln grew up among poor unlettered people of the Kentucky territory. His grandfather Abraham, a Virginia frontiersman of Quaker origin, had crossed the Alleghenies to Kentucky, where he was killed by Indians. His father Thomas, a carpenter, never learned to read or write. His mother, Nancy Hanks, a woman of gentle and mystical nature, unable to withstand the rigors of frontier life, died on October 5, 1818, when her son was nine years old. While Thomas whipsawed a log into planks for her coffin, young Abraham silently whittled wooden pegs to serve as nails. Together, the father and son buried the wife and mother in a clearing in the forest in an unmarked grave.

A year later the father remarried. A kindly widow with three children of her own, Sarah Bush Johnston brought order and warmth into the desolate log cabin by Pigeon Creek. In spite of the father's objections to book-learning, she sent young Abraham to a settlement school for a month or two at a time, whenever the boy could be spared from his chores. She was his "best friend in this world," her stepson said later. Though his total schooling amounted to less than a year, the boy learned to read and write and do arithmetic. The rest he taught himself. After the day's work in the woods, he would lie on the floor of the cabin in front of an open fire and study the few worn books which were his best possessions. His whole library in his youth consisted of *Pilgrim's Progress, Robinson Crusoe, Aesop's Fables,* a history of the United States, and a biography of George Washington.

At 16, young Abe was already known in the backwoods for his strength, his gift of speech, his quips and his funny stories. A tall, dark, angular youth who did odd jobs for anyone who would hire him, he could sink an ax deeper into wood and strike a heavier blow with a maul hammer than anyone else in the area. At 18, he was six feet four inches tall and weighed nearly two hundred pounds. "He looked as if he had been rough-hewn with an ax and needed smoothing with a jack plane," said Thomas Lincoln.

The family pulled up stakes and left Kentucky, moving farther west, to Indiana, then to Illinois. Young Lincoln drove the family wagon with a team of oxen along the rough frontier roads. Near Decatur, Illinois, he helped his father clear a patch of land and build a new log cabin. To fence 10 acres of land on the north side of the Sangamon River, he cut down walnut and locust trees and split them into rails. One summer, with the help of his cousin Dennis Hanks, he split three thousand rails.

At 21, he left his father's homestead, paddling a flatboat, and the waters of the Sangamon washed him into New Salem, a frontier village with some 20 cabins and 100 inhabitants, which became his home for the next five years. "A piece of floating driftwood," he called himself, "accidentally lodged at New Salem..." Farm hand, railsplitter, storekeeper, clerk at the election polls, postmaster, surveyor—he did whatever came his way. His ability as a storyteller, his native wit and kindliness, won him devoted friends.

When his boss, Denton Offutt, boasted that his new clerk could "outrun, whip, or throw down any man in Sangamon County," the terrors of the country-

*The birthplace of Abraham Lincoln. The little log cabin is now preserved near Hodgenville, Kentucky.*

*Sarah Bush Lincoln, Lincoln's adored step mother.*

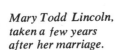

*Mary Todd Lincoln, taken a few years after her marriage.*

side, the Clary Grove boys, challenged the newcomer. Young Lincoln fought their leader in a public wrestling match, defeated him, and won the admiration of the bullies.

In 1832, when the governor of Illinois called for volunteers to fight the Indians, 23-year-old Lincoln enlisted in the militia. The Clary Grove boys elected him their captain. Not finding any Indians, young Lincoln did his best to prevent his unruly men from making war on the pigs and chickens of the farms they passed.

Returning home, he ran for the Illinois Assembly. Though almost everyone in New Salem voted for "Honest Abe," he lost the county election that year. In 1834, however, he won and was re-elected to the Assembly three times. A close and thoughtful reader of borrowed books, he read Shakespeare and Burns, Voltaire and Paine, as part of his self-education. He studied Blackstone and mastered the fundamentals of law. With the help of his friend Mentor Graham, a village schoolmaster, he studied Euclid and learned the art of surveying. He took part in debates and developed skill as a speaker.

His deepest attachment in New Salem was said to have been Ann Rutledge, a lovely auburn-haired girl of 18 when Lincoln first met her. She was a descendant of the Rutledge who had signed the Declaration of Independence. Malaria came to New Salem in the spring of 1835, and Ann died of it. She was 22. For weeks young Lincoln roamed the countryside like one who had lost his reason. "The thought that the snows and rains fall upon her grave fills me with indescribable grief" he told friends who tried to console him.

Packing all his worldly goods in two saddle bags, he left New Salem and rode to Springfield, the state capital, some 20 miles away. He never returned to New Salem. Within a few years the village by the Sangamon turned into a ghost town, overgrown with weeds and flowers.

Admitted to the bar in 1837, Lincoln became a partner in a law office. Preparing cases for courts in 14 counties, he spent years as a circuit lawyer, riding on horseback from village to village across the Illinois prairies. He was out in all kinds of weather, on hazardous roads, in isolated sections. In time, the cases he prepared were models of clarity. He considered both sides in every case. His arguments were strong and convincing, for he never forgot the roots of justice in common sense.

In 1842, at the age of 33, he married Mary Todd, a buxom, high-tempered and ambitious belle from Lexington, Kentucky. Though Stephen A. Douglas had courted her, she preferred the ungainly Lincoln. After their marriage, Lincoln bought a frame house on Eighth Street in Springfield where he raised a family of four sons. A devoted father, a patient husband, he endured his wife's high temper. Impatient with his rustic manners, she resented his slow progress.

When Douglas was already a national figure, Lincoln was still a poor country lawyer who plodded along the muddy streets of Springfield, a satchel on one arm, an old shawl on his shoulders, wearing a tall hat in which he kept his legal papers. He chopped his own wood and curried his own horse. His friends avoided his snobbish wife. When someone asked him why the Todd name was spelled with a double *d*, Lincoln remarked that, while one *d* was good enough for God, the Todds needed two.

As a circuit lawyer, Lincoln spent half the year away from home. The people of the prairies came to love and respect the gaunt, weatherbeaten traveler in black who spoke their language and who could tell jokes better than anyone else. Behind his funny stories they felt his deep humanity, his abiding faith in justice and the rights of man.

Elected to Congress in 1846, Lincoln went to Washington with high hopes. He opposed the Mexican War and fought for a resolution to outlaw slavery in the capital, but the bill was defeated. At the end of his term, 40-year-old Lincoln was not re-elected. He applied without success for several federal posts. Returning to Springfield, he continued his life as before.

By the middle of the 19th century, the question of slavery had become the most controversial national issue. In 1854, Lincoln opposed the Kansas-Nebraska Act, an act sponsored by Stephen A. Douglas, which extended slavery into Kansas. In 1856, Lincoln was active at the first convention of the newly organized and then radical Republican Party. In 1858, he engaged in a series of eight debates with Senator Douglas. Before he delivered his "House Divided" speech, Lincoln discussed it with friends. One called it "way ahead of its time"; another said it meant political suicide for Lincoln. They advised him against delivering it. But Lincoln said, "This thing has been retarded long enough. If it is decreed that I should go down because of this speech, then let me go down linked to the truth." Next day, June 18, 1858, he declared his belief in public: "A house divided against itself cannot stand. This government cannot endure permanently half-slave and half-free. . . ." His stirring debates with Douglas brought national political attention to Lincoln.

When the Republican party met in Chicago in May, 1860, it nominated Lincoln for president on an anti-slavery platform. In the mud-slinging campaign that followed, the opposition decried Lincoln as "a nullity, a maker of clumsy jokes, a third-rate country lawyer who resembles a gorilla." Lincoln got only 40 per cent of the popular vote, but the Democrats were divided and Lincoln was elected by 180 electoral votes to 123. On December 20, 1860, South Carolina seceded from the United States, soon to be followed by six other southern states. Rather than accept President Lincoln and his platform, they would break up the Union. Lincoln's enemies in Washington threatened to seize the Capitol; they vowed he would never enter the White House alive.

When Lincoln left Springfield for his inaugural one morning in February, 1861, he said farewell to his neighbors from the platform of the train. "No one not in my situation can appreciate my feeling of sadness at this parting," he said. "To this place, and the kindness of these people, I owe everything. Here, I have lived a quarter of a century, and have passed from a young to an old man. Here my children have been born, and one is buried. I now leave, not knowing when or whether ever I may return. Pray for me...."

*The Lincoln family in 1861. Left to right: Mrs. Lincoln, Willie, Robert, Tad, and the President.*

In Washington, on March 4, 1861, a small crowd attended his inaugural. Stiff in his new black clothes, Lincoln stood in front of 83-year-old Chief Justice Taney, author of the Dred Scott decision. His left hand on the Bible, Lincoln solemnly swore to preserve, protect, and defend the Constitution. In his inaugural address, he spoke to the dissatisfied people of the South and pleaded for unity. "You have no oath registered in heaven to destroy the government. . . . We are not enemies, but friends. . . . Though passion may have strained, it must not break the bonds of our affection. The mystic chords of memory, stretching from every battlefield and patriot grave to every living heart and hearthstone all over this broad land will yet swell the chorus of Union when again touched, as surely they will be, by the better angels of our nature . . ."

Less than six weeks after his inaugural, southern troops attacked the federal garrison at Fort Sumter in South Carolina. Their bombardment began on April 12. They shot down the flag and took the fort. On April 15, Lincoln called for 75,000 volunteers. So began the American Civil War.

Lincoln stood at the helm through four years of bitter warfare between the people of America. At the time the country's total population was approximately 31 million, of whom 27 million were whites and 4 million Negroes. When they seceded, the Confederate states of the South demanded recognition as a new and independent nation, formed by revolution. Lincoln contended that they were individual rebels against the Union, which was permanent and "must be preserved." The contest was marked by bitter battles at Bull Run, Shiloh, Antietam; at Fredericksburg, Chancellorsville, Gettysburg; at Vicksburg, the Wilderness, Cold Harbor, Atlanta. Before the end of the war, more than two million troops were engaged and the appalling number of casualties exceeded 640,000.

Day after day, Lincoln faced agonizing problems; a man of peace, he made decisions of life and death. "In times like the present," he told Congress, "men should utter nothing for which they would not willingly be responsible through time and eternity." Amidst great trials, he preserved his sense of proportion. He saw an endless stream of petitioners at the White House; his doors were open to the people at all times. "They don't want much," he would say with a sad smile. "They get little, and I see them." When an old neighbor from Springfield asked him how it felt to be president, Lincoln answered, "You have heard about the man tarred and feathered and ridden out of town on a rail? When a man in the crowd asked him how he liked it, his reply was that if it weren't for the honor of the thing, he'd much rather walk."

Lincoln issued his Emancipation Proclamation on January 1, 1863, giving political freedom to some three million Negroes in the South. In effect, the Proclamation restored the anti-slavery clause which had been cut from the Declaration of Independence in 1776, at the insistence of South Carolina and Georgia. The Proclamation gave new strength to the Union; it changed world opinion decisively in favor of the liberating North.

In a major battle at Gettysburg, Pennsylvania, ending on July 3, 1863, the brilliant commander of the Confederate army, Robert E. Lee, was repulsed by the Army of the Potomac. On November 19, 1863, Lincoln attended the dedication of a new national cemetery at Gettysburg. After a formal oration by the principal speaker, Lincoln rose to add "half a dozen words of consecration." The short speech he made at Gettysburg, on a drizzly autumn morning to an almost apathetic crowd, has since become familiar in the schoolbooks. It has been called the greatest speech in American history.

The year 1864 was marked by some of the worst trials and reversals of the war. Lincoln called for 500,000 additional recruits, an unpopular measure. He did not expect to be re-elected. In his own party the leading Republicans were now for "anybody but Lincoln." The Democrats nominated George B. McClellan, a vainglorious general whom Lincoln had fired. Anticipating his own defeat at the polls, Lincoln made plans to cooperate with his successor. When nominated, Lincoln's chief observation was that "it is not best to swap horses while crossing the river," whereupon the campaign cry became "Don't swap horses!" In November he was re-elected by a majority of 212 electoral votes to 21 for McClellan.

In the meantime, General Philip Sheridan had moved into the South, occupying the fertile Shenandoah Valley. General William Sherman had taken Atlanta in September, burned the city, then started his famous march toward the sea with a force of 60,000. General U. S. Grant was starting his fifth drive against Lee at Richmond. The long bitter war was entering its final phase.

At his inaugural, on March 4, 1865, Lincoln reviewed the tragic years. "Both parties deprecated war, but one of them would rather make war than let the nation survive; and the other would accept war rather than let it perish. . . . Both read the same Bible and pray to the same God, and each invokes His aid against the other. It may seem strange that any man should dare to ask a just God's assistance in wringing their bread from the sweat of other men's faces. But let us judge not, that we be not judged. . . ."

The scourge of war was a punishment the country suffered for the offense of slavery, an offense which had to be removed. Lincoln was ready to forgive the rebels, to restore and rehabilitate the vanquished, to compensate the South for its losses.

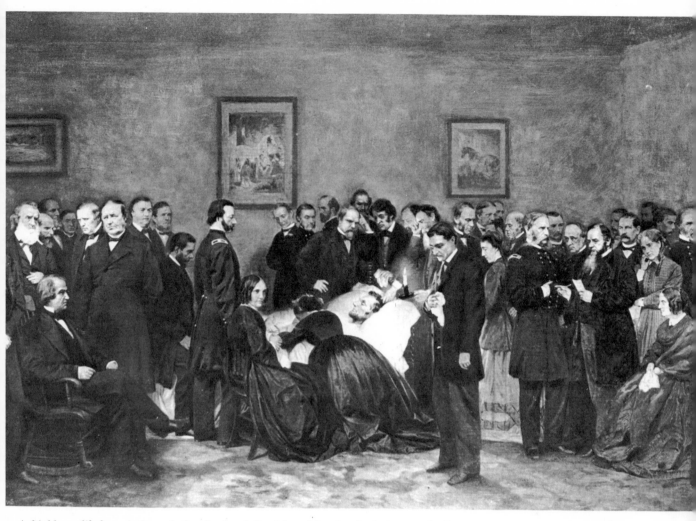

*A highly unlikely painting of the death of President Lincoln. It shows practically every important member of the administration. The room in which Lincoln died was very small, the bed so small he had to be laid on it diagonally.*

"With malice toward none, with charity for all, with firmness in the right, as God gives us to see the right, let us strive on to finish the work we are in—to bind up the nation's wounds; to care for him who shall have borne the battle, and for his widow and his orphans; to do all which may achieve and cherish a just and lasting peace among ourselves, and with all nations."

Less than a month after Lincoln's second inaugural, Grant took Richmond, Virginia, the capital of the Confederacy. On April 9, at Appomattox Court House, Lee surrendered to Grant with his remaining army of 27,000 starving men. Grant let the officers keep their swords; he let the men keep their horses and mules. "You'll need them for your spring plowing," he said. The liberated Negroes in the South were jubilant. They looked on "Father Abraham" as their great savior. In the city of Washington, people celebrated the end of the war. For days the capital was loud with bells, cannon salutes, parades, balls, and speeches.

On the evening of April 14, 1865, Lincoln attended a performance of *Our American Cousin* at Ford's Theater, a block from the White House. During the intermission he spoke with his wife of their plans for the future, of their hopes to travel abroad. "There is no place I should like to see so much as Jerusalem," were Lincoln's last words. At 10 o'clock, as the play began again, the door of their box was pushed open and John Wilkes Booth, a popular young actor of the day, pressed his single-shot derringer to the back of Lincoln's head and fired the bullet into his brain. Leaping to the stage, Booth, a Southern fanatic, brandished a dagger and shouted: *"Sic semper tyrannis —Virginia is avenged!"*

Lincoln was carried into a tailor's house across the street from the theater. His great gaunt body stretched on a bed too short for him, breathing laboriously through the night, he never regained consciousness. He died at 7:22 the next morning. At the end of the vigil, Secretary of War Edwin M. Stanton hoarsely spoke the words which were echoed by the nation, "Now he belongs to the ages."

# Andrew Johnson

**Born:** *December 29, 1808, Raleigh, North Carolina.* **Parents:** *Jacob and Mary Mcdonough Johnson.* **Education:** *none.* **Married:** *1827, Eliza McCardle (1810-76), five children.* **Career:** *tailor; mayor, Greenville (now spelled Greeneville), Tennessee, 1830-33; member, state constitutional convention, 1834; member, Tennessee legislature, 1835-37, 1839-41; state senator, 1841-43; U.S. representative, 1843-53; governor of Tennessee, 1853-57; U.S. senator, 1857-62, March 4 to July 31, 1875; military governor of Tennessee, 1862-64; vice-president, March 4 to April 15, 1865; seventeenth president, 1865-69.* **Died:** *July 31, 1875, Carter's Station, Tennessee; buried, Greeneville, Tennessee.*

As humble in origin as Jackson or Lincoln, Andrew Johnson was born in a poor white settlement in North Carolina. His father was a porter, his mother a maid in a tavern in Raleigh. When the boy was three, his father was drowned while trying to save another man's life. At 13, Andrew was apprenticed to a tailor. At 15, he ran away to become a journeyman in South Carolina. A notice appeared in the Raleigh *Gazette* offering a reward of ten dollars for the runaway apprentice. At 17, he settled in the hilly village of Greenville, Tennessee—the birthplace of David Crockett—and nailed a sign above his log cabin: A. JOHNSON, TAILOR. He made his own clothes for the rest of his life. A year later he married Eliza McCardle. A devoted and intelligent girl, she taught her husband to read and write. Joining the local Polemic Society, before long he became known as a debater.

A strong, energetic, self-reliant youth, swarthy as an Indian, at 20 Johnson was elected alderman on a workingmen's ticket. At 22, he was mayor of Greenville. A staunch Jacksonian Democrat, he served in the Tennessee assembly for six years, then in Congress, from 1843 to 1853. At 45, he was elected governor of Tennessee.

Elected to the U. S. Senate in 1857, he championed the rights of small farmers. He supported and pushed through the Homestead Act, which opened up vast tracts of public land for the benefit of the landless poor. Although a Southerner, he opposed secession. In Washington he stood alone against 22 Southern senators. He carried a brace of pistols and faced deadly threats when his own state seceded from the Union. In Tennessee he was hanged in effigy, his property confiscated, his family persecuted as "enemy aliens." In 1862, President Lincoln appointed him military governor of Tennessee. In 1864, Johnson was nominated vice-president with Lincoln on the National Union ticket. Six weeks after Lincoln's second inaugural, Johnson was president.

Instead of punishing the South, he pursued Lincoln's policy of conciliation and restoration. He issued his Proclamation of Amnesty, which offered a general pardon to rebels who returned their loyalty to the Union. He vetoed "reconstruction" measures which were intended to disenfranchise the Confederates and to turn four million Negroes into political pawns for Northern "carpetbaggers" and Southern "scalawags." The Ku-Klux Klan represented the South's efforts to terrorize the Negro and prevent him from voting. Johnson's conciliatory policy infuriated Congress, which was now controlled by radical Republicans bent on treating the South like a conquered country.

Blocked by Congress, Johnson went on a speaking tour of the East and the Middle West in an effort to vindicate his conduct. Wherever he spoke, he was shouted down, hooted, humiliated. A bold and pug-

*The United States Senate sitting as a court of impeachment for the trial of President Johnson.*

nacious man, Johnson held to his course. In Washington, he tried to dismiss from the cabinet his vengeful secretary of war, Edwin M. Stanton, and replace him with General Grant. But Stanton defied the president and refused to give up his office. Under pressure from Congress Grant withdrew.

Soon afterward, in a move planned by Thaddeus Stevens, a strong voice in the House of Representatives, the president was impeached for "high crimes and misdemeanors." No crimes were specified; the misdemeanor lay in Johnson's attempt to fire Stanton without consent of the Senate. The first and only such trial of a president in American history, the event roused the widest interest. The trial opened on March 5, 1868. Johnson did not attend. Expecting to be convicted, the "Tennessee Tailor" packed and prepared to leave the White House.

A majority of the senators, 35 in number, voted for his conviction; 19 voted for acquittal. The result was one less than the required two-thirds majority. Johnson was saved by a single vote.

During Johnson's administration his secretary of state, William H. Seward, bought Alaska from Russia for $7,200,000. Though the purchase added 4,000 miles of Pacific coastline and nearly 400 million acres of new territory to the United States at less than two cents an acre, it was called "Seward's Folly" at the time.

A man without a party, Johnson was not renominated in 1868. Seven years later he was elected to the Senate from Tennessee and took his seat in the same chamber in which he had been impeached. He was the first ex-president to become a senator. Vindicated finally, Johnson magnanimously offered his hand to a colleague who had voted for his conviction. In his only speech he pleaded, "Let peace and unison be restored to the land! May God bless this people and God save the Constitution!"

Johnson died on July 31, 1875. At his own wish he was buried with a copy of the Constitution he had so vigorously defended under his head and an American flag for a winding sheet.

# Ulysses S. Grant

**Born:** *April 27, 1822, Point Pleasant, Ohio.* **Parents:** *Jesse and Hannah Simpson Grant.* **Education:** *West Point, 1843.* **Married:** *1848, Julia Dent (1826-1902), four children.* **Career:** *army officer, 1843-54, 1861-68; farmer; real estate broker; store clerk; commander, Union armies, 1864-65; secretary of war, August, 1867 to January, 1868; eighteenth president, 1869-77.* **Died:** *July 23, 1885, Mt. McGregor, New York; buried, New York City.*

At the beginning of the Civil War Ulysses S. Grant was an unknown ex-army officer working in his father's leather shop in Galena, Illinois. Five years later he was the nation's most celebrated general, the first to wear four stars. The War had rescued him from obscurity.

Grant was born in 1822 at Point Pleasant, Ohio. As a boy he was fond of horses, wild or tame, but not

*General Grant at City Point, Virginia. A photograph of Grant was superimposed on one of the battlefield.*

of his father's tannery nor of schooling. In 1839, he went to the military academy at West Point, where he was an indifferent student. He hoped to get a post as assistant professor of mathematics at West Point and then to resign when his service was up and become a teacher at a college or university. Instead, he was sent to Jefferson Barracks in St. Louis after his graduation. In 1844, the Mexican War broke out and Grant went with his regiment to the southwestern frontier. Though he personally opposed the annexation of Texas and the fight with Mexico, he took part in the campaign. With Winfield Scott's army he fought in the battles at Vera Cruz, Molino del Rey, and Chapultepec. In the latter two he was promoted for bravery to first lieutenant and then to captain.

In spite of his distaste for it, the Mexican War was Grant's only real military proving ground. He learned what it was to wage war. During the Mexican War,

In the end Grant and the Union armies triumphed. The terrible war was finally ended. It was not in Grant to hate the vanquished South. With Lincoln he saw the ending of the war as the signal for the reunion of brothers, not as a cause for punishment and plunder of the South and its resources.

In 1866, Grant was made a full general, the first man in the history of the country to hold the four-star rank. He became somewhat reluctantly involved in politics when President Johnson appointed him to serve temporarily as secretary of war in place of Stanton, who declined to be fired, starting the row that led to Johnson's impeachment trial.

The Republican Convention in Chicago in 1868 unanimously nominated Grant as their presidential candidate. In the election the following fall, he won 214 electoral votes to New York Democrat Horatio Seymour's 80.

Grant was not a politician. As a president he is considered to have been below average in performance. He was largely a victim of his own political innocence. He appointed to high office men he trusted, and time and time again he found himself betrayed. His administration was marked by corruption and treachery.

During his second term, which he won by defeating Horace Greeley by an even larger margin than he had defeated Seymour, a financial collapse in Wall Street wiped out the holdings of some 23,000 small busi-

*On his world tour after leaving the White House, Grant was photographed with the Viceroy of China.*

too, Grant came to know many of the officers who would be fighting both for and against him in 15 years' time.

Grant remained in the army until 1854, when he resigned. He had married, had children and the army pay hardly supported his family while he was at one end of the country and they were at the other. Nothing Grant did was successful after he left the army. He tried farming near St. Louis but was obliged to sell his farm at an auction to pay his debts. He sold real estate, but again did not prosper. In 1860, he moved to Galena, Illinois, to clerk in his father's leather shop. At thirty-nine, Grant seemed to be a failure.

Then came the war. Rebuffed by the government in his bid for command of a regular army regiment, he accepted command of the 21st Illinois Regiment. Whatever Grant may have lacked in bearing or polish, he lacked nothing in determination. If he did not love a fight, he never shrank from one. When Lincoln was urged by others to get rid of Grant after the bloody battle at Shiloh, he replied: "I can't spare this man—he fights."

nesses. Grant was never implicated in any of the scandals that broke around his administration. When his second term expired, he made a world tour from Tokyo to London, and was acclaimed wherever he went as the hero of Appomattox.

In 1880, Old Guard Republicans tried to nominate Grant for a third term, but they failed. Persuaded to enter a Wall Street investment firm as a partner, Grant was left penniless when the firm collapsed in the panic of 1884. Grant's partner was convicted of fraud, but Grant himself was exonerated.

Living on borrowed money, Grant started to write his memoirs in an effort to support his family. Mark Twain had advanced Grant money and was to publish the memoirs when they were completed. Afflicted with cancer of the throat, Grant worked on doggedly. When he could no longer dictate to a secretary, Grant was forced to write in longhand. He died four days after he finished the second and final volume, on July 23, 1885. His *Memoirs* soon became a classic and brought to his family more money than he had earned in his lifetime.

*Grant, dying of cancer, writing his memoirs at his house at Mt. McGregor, near Saratoga Springs, New York.*

# Rutherford B. Hayes

**Born:** *October 4, 1822, Delaware, Ohio.* **Parents:** *Rutherford and Sophia Birchard Hayes.* **Education:** *Kenyon College, 1842; Harvard Law School, 1845.* **Married:** *1852, Lucy Ware Webb (1831-89), eight children.* **Career:** *lawyer; city solicitor of Cincinnati, 1857-59; army officer, 1861-65; U.S. representative, 1865-67; governor of Ohio, 1868-72, 1876-77; nineteenth president, 1877-81.* **Died:** *January 17, 1893, Fremont, Ohio.*

Posthumous son of an Ohio storekeeper, Rutherford B. Hayes was raised by a rich bachelor uncle, Sardis Birchard, who financed his education. Graduating from Kenyon College in 1842 as the youngest valedictorian, he studied at Harvard Law School, then practiced law in Cincinnati till the outbreak of the Civil War. Serving with the 23rd Ohio Volunteers, he was made a brigadier general in 1864, promoted to major general the following year. The same year he was nominated representative to Congress. Refusing to campaign, Hayes said: "An officer fit for duty, who at this crisis would abandon his post to electioneer for a seat in Congress, ought to be scalped." He took his seat in Congress in 1865. Two years later he was elected governor of Ohio. Defeated for Congress in 1872, he was re-elected governor in 1875. At the national convention held in Cincinnati in June, 1876, the Republicans nominated Hayes for the presidency.

When the returns were in, Hayes believed that he had lost the election to Samuel J. Tilden, reform governor of New York, by an electoral vote of 196 to 173. But Hayes' backers refused to admit defeat. They contested 22 electoral returns from South Carolina, Louisiana, and Florida. Congress appointed an Electoral Commission of 15, composed of five senators, five representatives, and five justices of the Supreme Court. Behind the scenes the Republicans made promises to withdraw federal troops from the South, and certain electors were persuaded to change their vote. When the final tallies were made, two days before the inaugural, the vote stood 185 to 184, in favor of Hayes. Though Tilden had been elected in November, he was too astonished or too proud to fight the reversal. Hayes lacked a popular majority by more than 300,000 votes and was made president by a margin of one electoral vote.

Pushed into the White House, Hayes acted contrary to expectations. Without consulting his backers, he

*Hayes was besieged by job seekers from the moment he took office. Below, a few in the White House lobby.*

*On September 28, 1878, President Hayes received Chun Lan Pin, the first Chinese Minister to the United States.*

selected a distinguished cabinet. Ignoring political spoilsmen and bosses, he tried to reform the civil service system, but was thwarted by Congress. "He serves his party best who serves his country best," he declared. Pursuing a policy of conciliation, he withdrew the last of the federal troops from the South, which led to the departure of the "carpetbaggers."

This helped to reunite the North and the South but left the Negro in the limbo of segregation.

Though his party called him a renegade, when Hayes left the White House he was more popular with the country at large than when he entered it. He declined to run for office in 1880, and retired completely from politics.

*The Hayes family in the library of the White House. The pianist is Carl Schurz, Secretary of the Interior.*

# James A. Garfield

**Born:** *November 19, 1831, Orange, Cuyahoga County, Ohio.* **Parents:** *Abram and Eliza Ballou Garfield.* **Education:** *Williams College, 1856.* **Married:** *1858, Lucretia Rudolph (1832-1918), seven children.* **Career:** *canal bargeman; farmer; carpenter; teacher; lawyer; member, Ohio senate, 1859; army officer, 1861-63; U.S. representative, 1863-80; elected to U.S. senate, 1880; twentieth president, March 4 to September 19, 1881.* **Died:** *September 19, 1881, Elberon, New Jersey; buried, Cleveland, Ohio.*

The twentieth president of the United States was the last one to be born in a log cabin and the only one who was both a canal bargeman and a professor of Greek and Latin before entering the White House. At 30, he had been the youngest brigadier general of the Civil War.

A descendant of Edward Garfield, who had settled in Massachusetts Bay Colony in 1630, he was born on a frontier farm in Cuyahoga County in Ohio. His father died fighting a forest fire when the boy was two. His widowed mother, Eliza Ballou, French Huguenot in origin, struggled hard to support her four small children. The youngest child, James, was his mother's favorite. This sturdy, blue-eyed, tow-headed boy was doing most of the chores on the family farm by the time he was 12. He was precocious in school, and an avid reader of history, poetry, and the Bible. His devoted mother hoped that he would become a teacher or a clergyman. At 15, he added to the family income by working as a carpenter's apprentice. At 16, he went to Cleveland and got a job on the Erie Canal; his first task was to drive mules along the tow-path of the Canal. Holding his own in a rough-and-tumble world, he was promoted to bargeman. Then he was stricken with a long illness.

Determined to get an education, at 20 he entered Hiram College and earned part of his expenses by working as the school janitor. He finished his schooling at Williams College, graduating with high honors in 1856. He returned to Hiram as professor of the classics, proved an able and popular teacher, and soon became president of the school. He later married one of his pupils, Lucretia Rudolph.

When President Lincoln called for volunteers in 1861, Garfield, a lifelong opponent of slavery, promptly marched with his regiment, the 42nd Ohio

*The Garfield children: left to right, Mollie, James, Harry, Abe, and Dan. Two other children had died.*

Volunteers. Many of his former students followed young Colonel Garfield. Distinguishing himself in campaigns at Sandy Hill, Corinth, Shiloh, and Chickamauga, at 31 Garfield was made a major general.

He was elected to Congress toward the end of 1863. Serving in the House during the next 17 years, he demonstrated superior abilities as an orator and legislator. Occasionally he would entertain his colleagues with a scholarly feat in ambidexterity: he would write in Greek with his left hand and, at the same time, in Latin with his right hand.

He was a dark-horse candidate at the Republican National Convention in Chicago in 1880 and was nominated on the thirty-sixth ballot, after both General Grant and James G. Blaine had been dropped. Garfield won the election against the Democratic candidate, General Winfield Scott Hancock, by a margin of only 9,464 votes of the more than nine million votes which were cast. The narrow margin indicates the divided state of the electorate.

After his inauguration Garfield was besieged by hungry office-seekers. During the weeks filled with interviews, he remarked somewhat ruefully, "I have been dealing all these years with ideas, and here I am dealing only with persons." On July 2, 1881, less than four months after his inaugural, he was waiting in the train depot in Washington with James G. Blaine, his secretary of state, on his way to deliver a commencement speech at Williams College. A disgruntled officeseeker, Charles J. Guiteau, stepped up with a small English bulldog pistol and fired two shots. Garfield fell forward on the floor.

For 79 days the entire country anxiously waited for news of their stricken president. On September 6, he was taken to Elberon, New Jersey. On September 19, he died at the age of 49.

*The Republican National Convention, Chicago, June 2, 1880. Garfield nominated General Sherman for the presidency.*

# Chester A. Arthur

**Born:** *October 5, 1830, Fairfield, Vermont.* **Parents:** *William and Malvina Stone Arthur.* **Education:** *Union College, 1848.* **Married:** *1859, Ellen Lewis Herndon (1837-80), three children.* **Career:** *teacher; lawyer; quartermaster-general of New York, 1862-63; collector of customs, port of New York, 1871-78; vice-president, March 4 to September 19, 1881; twenty-first president, 1881-85.* **Died:** *November 18, 1886, New York City; buried Albany, New York.*

Son of a Baptist clergyman from Belfast, Ireland, Chester Arthur was born and raised in the Green Mountain country in Vermont. His father, a strong abolitionist, influenced him in his later fight for equal rights for Negroes. At 17, Arthur graduated from Union College, where he had been a clever and popu-

lar debater and a member of almost every club and society on the campus, including Phi Beta Kappa. He taught school for a year, became principal of the academy at North Pownal, Vermont, where James Garfield—then a student at Williams College—taught penmanship during summer vacations.

After studying law, Arthur established himself as a successful lawyer in New York. During the Civil War he was appointed the state's quartermaster-general and made a good record. After the war he returned to his lucrative law practice. In 1871, President Grant appointed him collector of the port of New York. While in this office Arthur was in close association with the Republican boss of the state, Senator Roscoe Conkling.

At the Republican Convention in Chicago in 1880, Senator Conkling of New York had been promoting Grant for a third term. When Garfield was nominated, party leaders appeased the powerful senator by allowing him to name Garfield's running mate. Conkling chose his protege Chester Arthur who, as collector of the port of New York, had been a second-hand dispenser of political patronage in New York for the past 10 years. Arthur had been ousted from this job in 1878 by President Hayes in a house-cleaning program.

A tall handsome man of imposing appearance, the glass of fashion, Arthur was the most stylishly attired president since Martin Van Buren. Unlike the austere Hayes, he enjoyed high living and entertained lavishly. The White House was too gloomy and inconvenient for his taste, and he refused to live in the Executive Mansion until extensive renovations were carried out.

Conkling and his cronies were jubilant when Arthur was suddenly thrust into the presidency. They expected a quick return to the spoils system and easy morality of the Grant administration.

But Arthur had a mind of his own and he did not follow the style expected of him by his party. Breaking with Senator Conkling, he refused to indulge political spoilsmen. Instead, he carried out civil service reforms, establishing the merit system of competitive tests for the federal jobs. He did his best to give the country an honest and efficient administration.

Arthur's administration was a time of huge industrial expansion and wealth, and he insisted that the increased government revenues be used to reduce the national debt and rebuild the obsolete navy. Although he had alienated the politicians, he won the respect of many citizens in his short term. "It would be hard to better President Arthur's administration," said Mark Twain.

Having lost his party's support, and doing nothing to promote his candidacy, Arthur was not nominated in 1884. He died of apoplexy at 56, less than two years after he left the White House.

A GRAND SHAKESPERIAN REVIVAL
(Which We Have But Little Hope of Seeing on the Stage of the National Capital.)

*A contemporary cartoon showing Arthur with Grant, Gould, Vanderbilt, and Senator Conkling.*

*In 1884, President Arthur visited Newport, Rhode Island, the nation's most fashionable resort.*

# Grover Cleveland

**Born:** *March 18, 1837, Caldwell, New Jersey.* **Parents:** *Richard Falley and Anna Neal Cleveland.* **Education:** *common school.* **Married:** *1886, Frances Folsom (1864-1947), five children.* **Career:** *store clerk; teacher; lawyer; assistant district attorney, Erie County, New York, 1863-65; sheriff, Erie County, 1871-73; mayor of Buffalo, New York, 1882; governor of New York, 1883-85; twenty-second president, 1885-89; twenty-fourth president, 1893-97.* **Died:** *June 24, 1908, Princeton, New Jersey.*

The first Democratic president since the Civil War, Grover Cleveland was a huge, stubborn, courageous and independent champion of the people who fought corruption in government and whose consistent rule of conduct was, "A public office is a public trust." At 44, he was "veto mayor" of Buffalo, almost unknown; at 48, he was in the White House.

His election was closely contested in the presidential race of 1884, one of the most bitter in American history. His rival, James G. Blaine of Maine, a perennial presidential aspirant, was dubbed the "Plumed Knight" of the Republican party by Ralph G. Ingersoll. At a reception for Blaine, attended by six hundred clergymen in a Fifth Avenue hotel, a spokesman for one delegation, Reverend Samuel Burchard, committed a blunder which had wide repercussions. Wishing Blaine success, the Reverend declared fervently: "You must be elected, Mr. Blaine, to save this country from going down the road to hell through rum, Romanism, and rebellion!" The press played up the statement, which alienated many Roman Catholic voters in New York and helped swing the election to Cleveland. He was elected by the narrow margin of 23,005 popular votes over Blaine and by an electoral vote of 219 to 182.

Born in Caldwell, New Jersey, Stephen Grover Cleveland was the son of an impoverished Presbyterian minister. One of his ancestors, General Moses Cleveland, gave the city by Lake Erie its name. His mother, born in Baltimore, was of Irish origin. At 14, Grover was living in Clinton, New York, in his father's parsonage. He intended to enter Hamilton College, but his family's financial circumstances obliged him to change his plans. At 16, he was employed as a clerk and assistant teacher in an asylum for the blind in

*In the dirtiest political campaign in U.S. history, Cleveland snatched the presidency from James G. Blaine.*

New York City. At 18, he resolved to go "out West" and got as far as Buffalo, where he helped an uncle compile a reference work, *The American Herd-Book*. He also studied law and was admitted to the bar in 1859, at the age of 22. In 1871, he was sheriff of Erie County; in 1882, mayor of Buffalo; a year later, governor of New York.

A man of character, he was known for his ability to say "no" to Tammany Hall politicians. He exercised his veto repeatedly and turned down proposals with such annotations as "barefaced jobbery," "unblushing peculation," " . . . of all the defective and shabby legislation which has been presented to me, this is the worst and most inexcusable." His conduct as "veto governor" won the approval of independent voters, known as "Mugwumps." "We love him for the enemies he has made," said one who urged his nomination for the presidency in 1884.

In the White House, a massive, bull-necked bachelor who weighed 260 pounds, "Uncle Jumbo" was one of the most industrious and hardest-working chief executives, often staying up till 2 A.M. working on problems. "He would rather do something badly for himself," said Samuel Tilden, "than have somebody else do it well." Toward the end of his term, on the eve

*Cleveland entered the White House a bachelor, but in the second year of his first term he married Frances Folsom, who was twenty-seven years his junior. He was the first and only president to be married in the White House.*

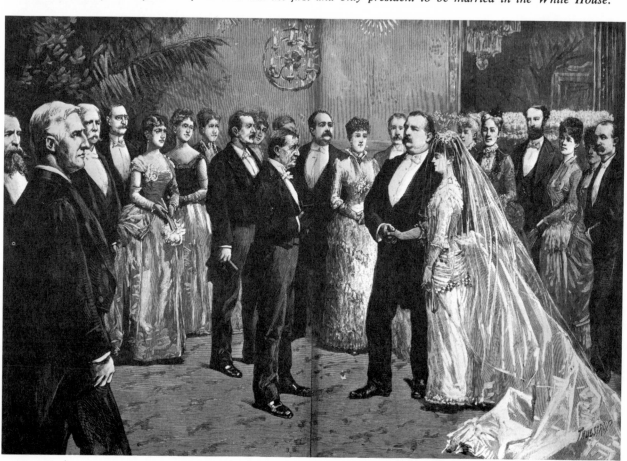

*Ex-President Cleveland with his wife and family at their home in Princeton, New Jersey.*

of the election of 1888, he did not hesitate to pursue a highly unpopular course, sending a message to Congress in which he firmly advocated reduction of the high tariff. "It is a condition which confronts us," Cleveland declared, "not a theory." His message was a challenge to big business interests which favored a high protective tariff. In his crusade for responsible government, Cleveland fought a hostile Congress with his favorite weapon—the veto.

He lost the 1888 election to Benjamin Harrison. In the second year of his administration, Cleveland had married Frances Folsom, the 21-year-old daughter of one of his former law partners. Before leaving the White House on March 4, 1889, an hour before the Harrisons moved in, Mrs. Cleveland is said to have told the staff: "Take good care of the furniture . . . We are coming back just four years from to-day." Her prediction came true. Exactly four years later, on March 4, 1893, the Clevelands were back in the White House. Cleveland had been elected in a sweeping victory of 277 electoral votes against 145 for Harrison. No other once-defeated president had ever been able to duplicate Cleveland's triumph.

His second administration was troubled by a serious nation-wide economic depression set off by the Panic of 1893 and marked by hundreds of bank failures, thousands of business bankruptcies, farm foreclosures, and the largest number of unemployed in the country's history. In the great Pullman strike of 1894, young Eugene V. Debs organized the railroad workers and was jailed for contempt of court. Cleveland called out federal troops to put down the Pullman strike. When Governor John Altgeld of Illinois protested, Cleveland said: "If it takes the entire army and navy of the United States to deliver a postal card in Chicago, that card will be delivered." His conduct in the Pullman strike lost him labor's support.

The distress and discontent of the farmers found voice in the new and radical Populist party, spearheaded by the militant young editor, William Jennings Bryan of Nebraska. An eloquent orator, Bryan fought against "Eastern plutocracy," against the gold standard and in favor of free silver coinage. In 1896, at the age of 36, Bryan was nominated for president by the Democrats, who had adopted much of the Populist party's program.

After leaving the White House, Cleveland retired to his home in Princeton, New Jersey, where he died in 1908. His last reported words were: "I have tried so hard to do the right."

# Benjamin Harrison

**Born:** *August 20, 1833, North Bend, Ohio.* **Parents:** *John Scott and Elizabeth Irwin Harrison.* **Education:** *Miami University, 1852.* **Married:** *1853, Caroline Lavinia Scott (1832-92), two children; 1896, Mrs. Mary Scott Lord Dimmick (1858-1948), one child.* **Career:** *lawyer; city attorney, 1852-60; reporter of the Supreme Court of Indiana, 1860-61, 1864-68; army officer, 1862-65; U.S. senator, 1881-87; twenty-third president, 1889-93.* **Died:** *March 13, 1901, Indianapolis, Indiana.*

Born on the family homestead at North Bend, Ohio, Benjamin Harrison was the great-grandson of Colonel Benjamin Harrison of Virginia, who had signed the Declaration of Independence. His grandfather, William Henry Harrison, was the ninth president, his father, John Scott Harrison, a congressman.

After graduating from a small Ohio college in 1852, young Harrison studied law in Cincinnati. His first job was as a court crier in Indianapolis for $2.50 a day. During the next 20 years he served as court reporter, city attorney, and colonel of the 70th Indiana Volunteers in the Civil War. He ran for governor of Indiana in 1876 but was defeated. He served one term in the U. S. Senate and was not re-elected. When he returned home in 1887, he called himself "a dead duck" and considered his political career finished.

Next year, at the Republican Convention in Chicago, he was chosen to run against Grover Cleveland by big businessmen who wanted a high protective tariff. They contributed the biggest campaign fund on record to secure Harrison's election. *"A surplus is*

these originated with the President. As in the case of other weak presidents, Congress seized the reins of leadership. Throughout his term, Harrison remained aloof from the problems of the nation.

In 1889 the Oklahoma territory was thrown open to the public for settlement, and six new states had joined the union by the end of Harrison's term—more than in any other administration.

Though no scandals were uncovered during the Harrison administration, it remained responsive to "special interests." The prosperity promised by the Republicans, however, failed to arrive. Renominated in 1892, Harrison lost the election decisively to Grover Cleveland, who received 277 electoral votes against 145 for Harrison.

A cautious, frigid, unimaginative man, Harrison retired from the political scene. He emerged in 1899 as a delegate to the peace conference at The Hague. He died two years later in Indianapolis, at the age of 67.

*Harrison's first wife, Caroline Scott. She died a few months before her husband left the White House.*

*The inauguration of President Harrison, March 9, 1889, on the steps of the Capitol.*

*easier to handle than a deficit,"* was the Republican slogan. Although Cleveland won the popular vote by almost 100,000, Harrison won the electoral vote, 233 to 168.

The new administration pushed through the highest protective tariff thus far enacted. Congress adopted the first billion-dollar budget in American history. The Treasury surplus of $97 million was voted in pensions to Northern veterans of the Civil War. The Sherman Antitrust Act was passed, to curtail the growth of huge monopolies and trusts. But none of

# William McKinley

**Born:** *January 29, 1843, Niles, Ohio.* **Parents:** *William and Nancy Campbell Allison McKinley.* **Education:** *Allegheny College.* **Married:** *1871, Ida Saxton (1847-1907), two children.* **Career:** *teacher; lawyer; Union army, 1861-65; prosecuting attorney, Stark County, Ohio, 1869-71; U.S. representative, 1877-83, 1885-91; governor of Ohio, 1892-96; twenty-fifth president, 1897-1901.* **Died:** *September 14, 1901, Buffalo, New York; buried, Canton, Ohio.*

"He was destined for a statue in the park and was practicing the pose for it," wrote William Allen White, editor of the Emporia *Gazette,* after an interview with President McKinley. The fifth Ohio-born Republican to enter the White House within 30 years, McKinley stood for the gold standard and the "full dinner pail." He won the race in 1896 against the crusading

Democratic candidate, William Jennings Bryan, in the most turbulent election campaign since the Civil War. Though personally opposed to intervention in Cuba —"McKinley has no more backbone than a chocolate éclair," exclaimed Theodore Roosevelt—he was persuaded to declare war on Spain in April, 1898. A reluctant commander-in-chief in the ten-week war to follow, he saw the United States assume the "white man's burden," taking over such far-flung islands as Puerto Rico and the Philippines and becoming a world power with overseas possessions.

Son of a foundryman and blast furnace operator, William McKinley was born in Niles, Ohio, the third youngest in a family of nine children. He was a junior in Allegheny College when poor health forced him to withdraw. He taught school for a while and was a post office clerk in Poland, Ohio, when the Civil War broke out. McKinley enlisted as a private in the 23rd Ohio Volunteers; Rutherford B. Hayes was his commanding officer. Serving with distinction, McKinley rose from private to major within four years. After the war he studied law and entered local politics. At 34, he was elected to Congress, where he served, except for one term, for the next 14 years and sponsored high-tariff bills. Elected governor of Ohio in 1891, and again in 1893, he did much to improve Ohio's roads and canals and public institutions.

In 1896, the Republicans needed a strong candidate against Bryan, the 36-year-old "Boy Orator of the Platte," who was tramping the country in an 18,000-mile campaign "to end the rule of the rich." McKinley's chief backer was Senator Mark Hanna, a rich industrialist from Ohio who built up a huge "war chest" for McKinley and promoted him with the party slogan *"Elect McKinley, Advance Agent of Prosperity."* During the campaign, McKinley, devoted to his invalid wife, stayed home and conducted a back-porch campaign, promising the return of the "full dinner pail." McKinley was elected by a popular vote of 7,104,779 to 6,502,925 for Bryan, and an electoral vote of 271 to 176.

As president, McKinley preserved the gold standard, maintained high-tariff protection, and pursued the "Open Door" policy of equal trading rights for all nations in China. The big event of his administration was the Spanish-American War, which started with the rebellion of Cubans against their Spanish rulers.

To avoid war, McKinley negotiated with Spain and secured the removal of the ruthless governor in Cuba. In February, 1898, to protect American lives and property in Cuba he sent a single battleship, the *Maine,* to Havana. When the ship was blown up by a submarine mine which killed 266 Americans, public resentment reached the fever point, and "Remember the Maine!" became the daily battle slogan on the mastheads of the nation's newspapers. On April 11,

1898, McKinley asked Congress to declare war "in the name of humanity, in the name of civilization, on behalf of endangered American interests."

In the course of the next 10 weeks, 40-year-old Theodore Roosevelt resigned his post as assistant secretary of the navy to lead his "Rough Riders" in a cavalry charge up San Juan Hill; General Nelson Miles captured Puerto Rico; Commodore George Dewey steamed into Manila with six warships and took the Philippines without losing a ship or a man. Spain asked for an armistice. In the peace treaty, signed in Paris on December 10, 1898, Spain ceded Puerto Rico, Guam, and the Philippines to the United States. Cuba was granted her independence. The same year the United States annexed Hawaii.

With Bryan as their candidate again in 1900, the Democrats unfurled banners with such party slogans as *"A Republic Can Have No Colonies,"* and *"Flag Of a Republic Forever, Of an Empire Never."* But McKinley was re-elected by an electoral vote of 292 to 155, with Theodore Roosevelt as his running mate.

Six months after his second inaugural, McKinley was attending the Pan-American Exposition in Buffalo, New York, when a young man stepped up as if to greet him. His right hand wrapped in a handkerchief to conceal his gun, Leon Czolgosz, a Chicago-born anarchist, fired two bullets into McKinley. The president was rushed to an emergency hospital where surgeons immediately operated. For a time he rallied

*McKinley refused a nationwide tour when he was nominated. He campaigned from his home in Canton, Ohio.*

and thanksgiving services were held throughout the country to celebrate his recovery. Then, on the eighth day, his heart began to fail. McKinley knew that he was sinking. "It is useless, gentlemen," he told the doctors. "I think we ought to have a prayer." Early on the morning of September 14, 1901, he died.

*A special funeral train took the President's body from Buffalo to Washington and then to Canton for burial.*

# Theodore Roosevelt

**Born:** *October 27, 1858, New York City.* **Parents:** *Theodore and Martha Bulloch Roosevelt.* **Education:** *Harvard, 1880.* **Married:** *1880, Alice Hathaway Lee (1861-84), one child; 1886, Edith Kermit Carow (1861-1948), five children.* **Career:** *author; rancher; explorer; member, New York legislature, 1882-84; member, U.S. Civil Service Commission, 1889-95; president, New York City police commission, 1895-97; assistant secretary of the navy, 1897-98; army officer, 1898; governor of New York, 1899-1901; vice-president, March 4 to September 14, 1901; twenty-sixth president, 1901-09. Received Nobel peace prize for 1906.* **Died:** *January 6, 1919, Sagamore Hill, Oyster Bay, New York.*

Born in New York City in the narrow three-story brick family residence at 28 East 20th Street, Theodore Roosevelt was a seventh-generation New Yorker. Of Dutch, French Huguenot, and Scotch-Irish origins, his first American ancestor was Claes Martenszen Van Rosenvelt, an immigrant from Holland who settled in New York in 1650. Theodore's father was a success-

ful glass merchant, a banker, a rich and prominent civic leader.

"Having been a sickly boy with no natural bodily prowess, I was at first quite unable to hold my own. . . ." he later reported in his *Autobiography*. "I was nervous and timid. Yet from reading of the people I admired, I felt a great admiration for men who were fearless and who could hold their own in the world, and I had a great desire to be like them."

One of his first challenges was to build up his physique. He did so with a will, practicing at home with Indian clubs and iron bars till he had, literally, transformed his body. At 16, he entered Harvard, became a student of natural sciences, editor of the *Advocate,* and a member of Phi Beta Kappa. "My ambition was to become a scientific man." Though his defective eyes limited his work with the microscope, he remained an enthusiastic amateur naturalist throughout his life.

Graduating from Harvard in 1880, he attended Columbia Law School, married Alice Hathaway Lee, and served from 1882 to 1884 in the New York State Assembly. Then a tragic blow struck him. His beautiful young bride and his mother both died within 24 hours. In an effort to recover, 25-year-old Roosevelt left New York and went into ranching in the Bad Lands of the Dakota Territory. Working with cowboys in the land of the long-horned cattle, he made friends with hundreds of westerners. From the spirit of the frontier he drew fresh faith and confidence in life.

Back in New York in 1886, he ran for mayor at the age of 28 and was defeated. Ten years later he was president of the New York City Police Commission. Ignoring the threats of political bosses, he fought against the spoils system, fired crooked policemen, rounded up gangsters, and cleaned up the city. Within a year, "Teddy the Scorcher" had become a favorite of cartoonists and a hero of New York City.

Appointed by McKinley as assistant secretary of the navy in 1897, he urged the building of a strong navy. "Build a battleship in every creek!" he cried when Spain was threatening to crush Cuba's struggle for independence. When the *Maine* was sunk in the harbor of Havana in 1898, Roosevelt resigned his office. Raising a company of volunteers, he led his Rough Riders in the celebrated charge up San Juan Hill and was promoted to colonel for his conduct in the field. In ten weeks the Spanish-American War was fought and won. Roosevelt was a national hero, a position he shared with Admiral Dewey, who had taken Manila.

Elected to the governorship of New York, the Rough Rider continued to wage his strenuous battle against corruption and injustice. In 1900, Republican party bosses backed his selection as vice-president, an office which was considered a political grave-yard. When Mark Hanna heard of McKinley's death, he exclaimed, "That damned cowboy is in the White House!"

With great vigor, President Roosevelt pushed through his "Square Deal" program. He broke up giant trusts, hunted for "malefactors of great wealth," and prosecuted monopolies in oil, sugar, meat packing, and tobacco. He launched the Department of Labor and the Department of Commerce and sponsored the Workmen's Compensation Act, the Pure Foods and Drug Act, and the Reclamation Act, which involved the building of great dams to irrigate the arid West. As part of his national conservation program, he fought for the preservation of forests and scenic areas, game and wildlife refuges; he launched the construction of 51 national bird sanctuaries.

Elected in his own right in 1904, by an electoral vote of 336 to 140, he continued his vigorous policies. When German imperialists penetrated Brazil, then blockaded Venezuela, Roosevelt sent a warning to Kaiser Wilhelm II. The warning was ignored. Roosevelt assembled the fleet under Admiral Dewey and sent the Kaiser an ultimatum: "Withdraw from Venezuela or we open fire." The Kaiser withdrew. "Speak softly and carry a big stick; you will go far," was Roosevelt's favorite proverb.

In 1905, asked to mediate in the war between Russia and Japan, he met in New Hampshire with delegates from both countries and negotiated an acceptable peace treaty. He was the first to use the Hague Court of International Arbitration. Honored for his contributions to world peace, he was the first American to win a Nobel Prize, the peace prize of 1906.

*In 1885, on one of his western hunting trips, Roosevelt was photographed in full frontier regalia.*

*Colonel Roosevelt and his Rough Riders, photographed at the top of San Juan Hill after the famous victory.*

One of his major achievements was pushing through the completion of the Panama Canal. Determined to accomplish his goal and cutting corners to do so, he recognized the new-born Republic of Panama, and revived the tremendous project. "If I had followed traditional methods," he explained later, "we would have had a half a century of discussion, and then perhaps the Panama Canal. . . . I preferred that we should have the Panama Canal first and the half century of discussion afterward."

Within two weeks after leaving the White House, Roosevelt embarked on an expedition to Africa which lasted nearly a year. "My last chance to be a boy," confessed the 50-year-old ex-president. A big game hunter and naturalist, he shot lions, collected valuable specimens and sent them to the Smithsonian Institution. He toured Egypt, Europe, England. In Brazil he discovered the source of the River of Doubt, named Rio Roosevelt.

Back in America in 1912, displeased with President Taft, he split the Republicans and formed the Progressive party, with himself as presidential candidate. At the polls, Roosevelt received a popular vote higher than Taft's, but the split in the Republican party led to Woodrow Wilson's election.

When America entered World War I, Roosevelt asked President Wilson for permission to raise and lead a division of volunteers. But Wilson turned down the aging warrior. "I am the only one he has kept out of the war," Roosevelt observed. His four sons enlisted; two were wounded. His youngest son, Quentin, a pilot, was shot down in his plane in July, 1918, and was buried where he fell.

Six months later Theodore Roosevelt himself lay on his deathbed. "Both life and death are parts of the same great adventure," he remarked. He was buried on Sagamore Hill beside a bird sanctuary he had founded.

*The Roosevelt family: Kermit, Archie, the President, Ethel, Mrs. Roosevelt, Quentin, and Theodore, Jr.*

# William Howard Taft

**Born:** *September 15, 1857, Cincinnati, Ohio.*
**Parents:** *Alphonso and Louise Maria Torrey Taft.* **Education:** *Yale, 1878; Cincinnati Law School, 1880.* **Married:** *1886, Helen Herron (1861-1943), three children.* **Career:** *newspaper reporter; lawyer; assistant prosecuting attorney, Hamilton County, Ohio, 1881-83; U.S. collector of internal revenue, 1st Ohio district, 1882-83; assistant solicitor, Hamilton County, 1885-87; judge, Superior Court of Ohio, 1887-90; U.S. solicitor-general, 1890-92; U.S. circuit court judge, 1892-1900; professor and dean, law department, University of Cincinnati, 1896-1900; president, U.S. Philippine Commission, 1900-01; governor, Philippine Islands, 1901-04; secretary of war, 1904-08; provisional governor of Cuba, September 29 to October 13, 1906; twenty-seventh president, 1909-13; professor of law, Yale, 1913-21; chief justice, United States Supreme Court, 1921-30.* **Died:** *March 8, 1930, Washington, D.C.; buried, Arlington, Virginia.*

In contrast to the strenuous little Rough Rider, William Howard Taft was a quiet, bland, good-humored mountain of a man. He stood six feet two and weighed more than three hundred pounds. Physically, he was the largest man to fill the presidential boots. The only American to hold both the highest executive and highest judicial office, he filled both with dignity and competence.

His father, Alphonso Taft, had served in Grant's cabinet as secretary of war and as attorney general. Later, under President Arthur, he had been minister to Russia. His son William, a smiling roly-poly child, early acquired the nickname "Fatty." His playmates in Cincinnati, urging him to join them on fishing trips, would tease him, "If you can't walk, we'll roll you, old butter ball!" In a school play at Woodward High School, young Taft played the part of Sleeping Beauty. Wearing a nightgown and a wig of golden curls, posturing languidly, the fat boy convulsed his audience. At Yale, he played baseball and football. When he graduated, in the class of 1878, he stood second highest in scholarship.

After studying law in Cincinnati, he became court reporter for the local press. A jovial young giant of 23, he launched a crusade against corruption in the Ohio courts and helped to bring about lasting reforms. At 28, he married Helen Herron, daughter of a judge who had been a law partner of Rutherford B. Hayes. Progressing rapidly, by the time he was 35 Taft had risen from assistant district attorney to federal circuit judge. His wife had still greater ambitions for him, but his mother said, "His is a judicial mind; he loves the law." She warned her son against trying to become president.

When Spain ceded the Philippines to the United States, President McKinley chose Taft to govern the protectorate. Though he knew little about the distant Pacific islands, Taft left Cincinnati to serve as the first governor of the Philippines. Furnishing a model of enlightened administration, he set up free public schools, courts of justice, hospitals, a postal savings bank system. To negotiate a transfer of lands which had belonged to the Roman Catholic Church and which were claimed by the natives, Taft made a journey to Rome. He visited the pope and persuaded him to sell the disputed property. Congress voted to pay $7,239,000 for it.

While serving in the Philippines, Taft twice declined an office he most desired: a place on the bench of the Supreme Court. He felt that his first duty lay with the Filipinos, whom he called "my little brown brothers." He trained the most able natives in the principles of democratic government so that they could carry on independently the work he had begun. Concerned about Taft's health, Secretary of War Elihu Root cabled him for information. Taft answered: "I am

77

well. I rode 25 miles this morning on horseback." Root cabled again: "How is the horse?"

President Theodore Roosevelt called Taft home in 1904 to serve as secretary of war. Known for his abilities as a conciliator, Taft was sent to Cuba, then to Panama, then to Japan. In each place he carried out his mission as a mediator successfully. Roosevelt (who then considered him "the most lovable personality I have ever known") groomed him for the presidency and helped secure his election in 1908. Against William Jennings Bryan, the Democratic candidate, who was running for the third and last time, Taft got a popular vote of 7,678,908 to Bryan's 6,409,104, and an electoral vote of 321 to 162.

As president, Taft followed the Square Deal policies. He pushed through a number of anti-monopoly measures, sponsored the 16th and 17th amendments to the Constitution, established the Federal Children's Bureau, and introduced the national budget. Toward the end of his term, however, unable to deal firmly with factions in Congress, he antagonized progressives and alienated Roosevelt, who now called him "useless to the American people." In the next election Taft agreed to run, "to perform a public duty—to keep Roosevelt out of the White House."

In the campaign of 1912 Roosevelt blocked Taft's re-election by organizing the Progressive or "Bull Moose" party which split the Republican vote and led to the election of Woodrow Wilson, a Democrat. When he left the White House, Taft called it "the lonesomest place in the world." Unwilling to capitalize on his prestige as a former president, he refused lucrative offers. Instead, he taught law at Yale from 1913 to 1921. A supporter of Wilson, he advocated the League of Nations and served as an officer of the League to Enforce Peace. In 1921, President Harding appointed him Chief Justice of the Supreme Court.

Realizing his greatest ambition and enjoying the highest honor ever accorded an ex-president, Taft presided over the Supreme Court for nine years. He started his day at 5:15 each morning and carried out his duties with deep satisfaction. Resigning on account of illness in February, 1930, he died a month later and was buried in Arlington National Cemetery.

*President Taft and his sons. Charles and Robert. The latter became a famous United States senator from Ohio.*

# Woodrow Wilson

**Born:** *December 28, 1856, Staunton, Virginia.*
**Parents:** *Joseph Ruggles and Janet (Jessie) Woodrow Wilson.* **Education:** *Princeton, A.B., 1879; A.M., 1882; University of Virginia Law School, 1879-81; Ph.D., Johns Hopkins, 1886.* **Married:** *1885, Ellen Louise Axson (1860-1914), three children; 1915, Mrs. Edith Bolling Galt (1872-1961), no children.* **Career:** *lawyer; teacher; author; president, Princeton, 1902-10; governor of New Jersey, 1911-13; twenty-eighth president, 1913-21. Received Nobel peace prize for 1919.*
**Died:** *February 3, 1924, Washington, D.C.*

Son of a Calvinist clergyman, grandson of a printer from Ireland, Woodrow Wilson was a schoolmaster by vocation, a scholar by inclination, a moralist by temperament. He taught history in the classroom till he was 50. Then he became a maker of history. Commander-in-chief in a war to end war, he fought to es-

tablish the League of Nations. He spent the last 10 years of his life expounding to mankind the principles of morality in government.

He left Princeton in 1910 to enter politics. Running on a reform platform, he was elected governor of New Jersey. The record he made cleaning up corruption in New Jersey won him national notice. In 1912, at the Democratic convention in Baltimore, he was nominated for the presidency on the 46th ballot. He won the election—receiving 435 electoral votes to 88 for Theodore Roosevelt and 8 for Taft—and left New Jersey to take his place at what he called "the most perilous helm in Christendom."

Launching his "New Freedom" program, he carried out a number of reforms. A specialist in the science of government, he was the first president with an earned Ph.D. Author of such works as *Constitutional Government, A History of the American People,* and a biography of George Washington, he spoke with authority when he said, "The president is at liberty, both in law and conscience, to be as big a man as he can." Academically better trained than any of his predecessors, Wilson surrounded himself with the best available advisers. "I not only use all the brains I have," he remarked, "but all I can borrow." Advocating and explaining his measures, he frequently spoke before Congress, a practice which had been abandoned since the days of John Adams.

An enemy of special privilege, Wilson curbed the power of monopolies, reduced the tariff, and encouraged free trade. He curtailed the power of big banking interests by establishing the Federal Reserve System, an act which helped the growth of the South and the West. To eliminate unfair business practices, he set up the Federal Trade Commission. To safeguard labor and agriculture and the health of the people, he sponsored such measures as the Farm Loan Act, the Child Labor Act, and the Pure Food Act.

In 1914, World War I broke out in Europe. In 1916, Wilson was re-elected—in a close contest with Chief Justice Charles Evans Hughes—on his promise to keep America out of the war. But in a world threatened by an aggressive Germany, America could not maintain her "splendid isolation." As the situation came near the breaking point, Wilson, determined to keep his promise, entered a period of agonizing trial. One who knew him well, Colonel Edward House, wrote in his diary in 1916: "His burdens are heavier than any president's since Lincoln. . . . He is one of the most difficult and complex characters I have ever known. . . . I believe he will live in history as one of the greatest presidents, if not the greatest."

Pursuing a policy of terrorizing the world, Germany launched unrestricted submarine warfare in the Atlantic in 1917. A number of American ships were sunk. On Monday, April 2, 1917, less than five

79

months after his re-election, Wilson appeared before Congress. "Aware of the solemn and even tragical character of the step I am taking," Wilson declared Germany's recent course of action to be an undeclared war against the United States. "It is a fearful thing to lead this great peaceful people into war. . . . But the right is more precious than peace. . . . The world must be made safe for democracy." Four days later, on Good Friday, Congress declared war against Germany.

Wilson spearheaded the Great Crusade. The whole country was mobilized; shipyards and factories worked around the clock; the nation went on an austerity schedule to send food and supplies overseas. The emergency powers conferred on Wilson by Congress made him, in his own words, "the greatest autocrat in history." Time was of the utmost importance, for Germany seemed on the verge of conquering Europe. "Our backs are to the wall," the Allies appealed to Wilson. Lloyd George, the British prime minister, said: "It is a race between Hindenburg and Wilson."

In June, 1917, General John Pershing sailed for Europe with American troops. By the middle of the next year thousands of Americans had been killed in Belleau Wood, at Château-Thierry, at Saint-Mihiel, in the Argonne Forest. They turned the tide of battle and forced a seemingly invincible enemy to retreat and then to capitulate. On November 11, 1918, the armistice was signed.

Nearly a year before the war ended, Wilson published the terms of the treaty which he felt must follow. His 14-point program included open covenants of peace between the nations, freedom of the seas, fair treatment of colonial claims, the right to self-determination, the removal of economic barriers, reduction of armaments, and most important, a League of Nations to maintain world peace.

The League represented Wilson's great vision. It embodied his hope to free mankind forever from the scourge of war. When he left for France in December, 1918, as head of the American delegation to the peace conference at Versailles, the long-suffering masses of Europe gave him a delirious welcome and hailed him as their messiah. But the diplomats at the

*The Wilson family in 1912: Margaret, Mrs. Wilson, Eleanor, and Jessie. Wilson was then governor of New Jersey.*

*The "Big Four" in Paris: Orlando of Italy, Lloyd George of England, Clemenceau of France, and President Wilson.*

peace conference were more concerned with punishing the aggressor than with removing the causes and preventing the recurrence of war. They cut and reduced Wilson's 14-point program. Wilson held firmly to his most cherished point. By his presence, his eloquence, his powers of persuasion, he achieved the formation of the League of Nations.

Returning to America in February, 1919, Wilson was met by enthusiastic crowds wherever he went. The majority in Congress were in favor of the League. Certain influential senators, however, such as Henry Cabot Lodge, Sr., William Borah, and Hiram Johnson, had reservations. They wanted changes in the details of the plan. They did not want the United States to become subject to the vetoes of other nations. Wilson refused to compromise.

His all-or-nothing attitude united the die-hard isolationists against him. Wilson then turned to the people for support and went on a speaking tour, addressing thousands in small towns throughout the Middle and Far West. He pleaded with the country to support

the League. In a last public speech at Pueblo, Colorado, on September 26, 1919, he asked the country to remember its dead sons and fathers and to safeguard its unborn. "My clients are the children; my clients are the next generation . . ." While speaking, he suffered a stroke which left him a paralytic invalid for the rest of his life.

The Senate voted on November 19, 1919, to enter the League of Nations, by 49 votes against 35. But the vote did not represent the required two-thirds majority—it fell short by seven—so the measure was defeated by a handful of "irreconcilables." Though most countries in Europe, Asia, and South America joined the League, the United States never did. "A little group of willful men, representing no opinion but their own," said Wilson, "have rendered the great government of the United States helpless and contemptible."

Wilson died in 1924, three years after he had left the White House. "Ideas live; men die," he said. His idea lives on in the United Nations.

81

# Warren G. Harding

**Born:** *November 2, 1865, Blooming Grove (now Corsica), Ohio.* **Parents:** *George Tryon and Phoebe Elizabeth Dickerson Harding.* **Education:** *Ohio Central, 1879-1882.* **Married:** *1891, Mrs. Florence Kling De Wolfe (1860-1924), no children.* **Career:** *teacher; newspaper reporter, editor and publisher; member, Ohio senate, 1900-04; lieutenant-governor, 1904-06; U.S. senator, 1915-21; twenty-ninth president, 1921-23.* **Died:** *August 2, 1923, San Francisco, California; buried, Marion, Ohio.*

Warren Harding was raised on his family's farm near Marion, Ohio. He played the alto horn in high school, learned the printer's trade, and taught school for one term. At 19, after managing a dance band, he became a reporter on the Marion *Star.* When the paper was on the verge of bankruptcy, he raised $300 and bought

it. He developed the *Star* into a popular local Republican party organ and remained its editor, owner, and publisher most of his life.

At 26, he married a divorced woman six years older than himself. Mrs. Harding was the daughter of the town's leading banker, a close student of astrology. She exerted considerable influence over her husband. Harding became an increasingly prosperous businessman. At 35, he entered local politics and became known as a good poker player, a vote-getter, a sonorous orator, and everybody's friend. In 1914, he was sent to Congress as senator from Ohio.

An Old Guard Republican, Senator Harding fought federal control of food and fuel, voted for anti-strike legislation, and firmly opposed the League of Nations as a threat to national sovereignty. At the Republican Convention in Chicago in June, 1920, his old friend and party boss, Harry M. Daugherty, pushed Harding to the front as presidential timber. On the tenth ballot, Harding was nominated, with Calvin Coolidge as his running mate. The Democratic candidates were James M. Cox and Franklin Delano Roosevelt.

Harding conducted his campaign from the front porch of his house in Marion and did not extend himself. He promised "a return to normalcy" and "an end to executive autocracy." The country at large, weary of Woodrow Wilson's austere moral leadership and ready to renew its isolation from world affairs, swept Harding into office with a plurality of seven million votes.

Though Harding's cabinet included several able men, he also picked men who proved unworthy. Corruption was in the air at the start of the Roaring Twenties. The government was active in the disposal of alien property worth millions of dollars, in the sale of surplus merchant ships, and in the management of rich oil lands. Opportunities for graft were plentiful.

Before long a series of scandals broke, involving members of the cabinet in charges of graft and bribery. The charges affected the secretary of the interior, Albert B. Fall; secretary of the navy, Edwin Denby; attorney general, Harry M. Daugherty; the head of the Veteran's Bureau; and agents of the department of justice. Fall resigned and was later sent to prison for his part in the Teapot Dome scandal, which involved the leasing, without competitive bidding, of the government-owned Teapot Dome oil reserve to persons from whom Fall had accepted bribes.

Deeply distressed, Harding went on a speaking tour and tried to vindicate himself before the people. Returning from a visit to Alaska in the summer of 1923, Harding fell ill and died suddenly on August 2.

Herbert Hoover, who was secretary of commerce in Harding's cabinet, said later: "Harding has been betrayed by a few men whom he had trusted, by men who, he believed, were his devoted friends."

*Harding and his cabinet in 1921. Seated beside the President are (left) Secretary of State Charles Evans Hughes and (right) Vice-President Coolidge. Secretary of Commerce Herbert Hoover is second from right in second row.*

*Harding on his Alaskan tour, with a team of polar huskies who pulled mail sleds north of the 54th parallel.*

# Calvin Coolidge

**Born:** *July 4, 1872, Plymouth, Vermont.* **Parents:** *John Calvin and Victoria Josephine Moor Coolidge.* **Education:** *Amherst, 1895.* **Married:** *1905, Grace Anna Goodhue (1879-1957), two children.* **Career:** *lawyer; member, city council, Northampton, Massachusetts, 1899-1900; city solicitor, 1900-01; clerk, county courts, 1903-04; member, Massachusetts house of representatives, 1907-08; mayor of Northampton, 1910-11; member, Massachusetts senate, 1912-15; president, state senate, 1914-15; lieutenant-governor, 1916-18; governor, 1919-20; vice-president, 1921-23; thirtieth president, 1923-29.* **Died:** *January 5, 1933, Northampton, Massachusetts; buried, Plymouth, Vermont.*

When President Harding died in San Francisco, Vice-President Calvin Coolidge was spending the summer on the family farm at Plymouth Notch, Vermont, a tiny village in the foothills of the Green Mountain

country. His father woke his son in the middle of the night and quietly told him the news which had been relayed from California. The 51-year-old son quietly dressed and went downstairs into the parlor of the farmhouse.

"Are you still a notary public?" he asked his old father.

"Yes."

"Then you will administer the oath."

So, at 3 A. M., by the light of a kerosene lamp, the father conducted a ceremony which was usually reserved for the chief justice of the Supreme Court. Placing his hand on the family Bible, the son solemnly pledged to uphold the Constitution. He signed the same oath George Washington had signed 134 years earlier. The father stamped the paper with his notary's seal and was the first to call his son "Mr. President."

A laconic Yankee with a dry sense of humor, Coolidge was the first New Englander to become president since Franklin Pierce. He was born on the Fourth of July. As a boy he spent his summers working in sawmills or logging. He was a quiet industrious lad in a frugal and taciturn community.

Attending Amherst, he won a prize for an essay on the causes of the American Revolution. After graduating with high honors, he entered law practice in Northampton, Massachusetts. In the next 20 years, "Silent Cal" served in 19 offices, from town councilman to state governor. Parsimonious in words and frugal with the public purse, he let his record speak for itself. He served in more elective offices than any other president.

The policemen of Boston went on a strike in 1919 because the police commissioner had refused to let them join the American Federation of Labor. When rioting followed and the city was threatened with a general strike, Governor Coolidge sent out the militia and put Boston under martial law. He sent a wire to Samuel Gompers, president of the A.F.L.: "There is no right to strike against the public safety by anybody, anywhere, anytime."

Though many thought that Coolidge had ruined himself politically by antagonizing labor, his firm stand and decisive action won him a national reputation and led to his nomination for vice-president.

The sixth vice-president to be elevated to the office by the death of the president, Coolidge cleaned up the scandals of the Harding administration. The oil lands, fraudulently sold, were restored to the federal government; the chief offenders were prosecuted. Through his quiet and efficient housecleaning Coolidge managed to save the Republican party from blame for the scandals.

Elected in his own right by a large majority in 1924, he carried on as before, while the post-war boom rose to new heights. "The business of America is business," said Coolidge. Cautious and frugal, he reduced the national debt by two billion dollars. He opposed the reduction of Europe's war debt: "They hired the money, didn't they?" He refused to sign the soldiers' bonus bill, which was then passed by Congress over his veto.

One of Coolidge's best-remembered remarks is what he told the press in the fall of 1927: "I do not choose to run for president in 1928." When he bowed out from the White House, he was more popular than when he entered it.

Retiring to Northampton, Coolidge wrote a daily newspaper column for a year. For his syndicated column of 200 words a day he was paid an annual salary of $200,000. He died in 1933, at the age of 60, and was buried at Plymouth, Vermont, the village of his birth.

*Below: President Coolidge on the White House lawn with a delegation of Indians from the Sioux Nation.*

*Above: Vice-President Coolidge working out in the gymnasium with the Indian clubs.*

The son of a Quaker blacksmith, Herbert Hoover was raised on a farm at West Branch, Iowa. Orphaned at eight, he went to live with relatives in Oregon. At 17, he entered Stanford University, where he majored in geology and mining engineering. He earned most of his tuition and living expenses. After graduation he worked as a laborer in a northern California mine for $2.50 a day. At 23, he was employed by an engineering firm in San Francisco. Within a short time he was entrusted with the task of setting up and operating gold mines in Australia and China. At 30, he had branch offices of his own throughout the world. At 40, he was a multimillionaire, a financier of mining properties around the globe.

When Belgium was confronted with the enormous problem of feeding and clothing ten million victims of the German invasion in 1914, Hoover undertook the task. An efficient administrator, he distributed more than five million tons of food, clothing, and medicines. Between 1917 and 1919 he organized and directed a vast rehabilitation program for war-torn Europe. He served without pay and gave part of his own fortune to help the needy.

In 1928, he was elected president by an electoral vote of 444 to 87, the largest majority accorded any president since George Washington. Then came the economic crash of 1929.

# Herbert Hoover

**Born:** *August 10, 1874, West Branch, Iowa,* **Parents:** *Jesse Clark and Hulda Randall Minthorn Hoover.* **Education:** *Stanford, 1895.* **Married:** *1899, Lou Henry (1875-1944), two children.* **Career:** *mining engineer; author; chairman, American Relief Committee, 1914-15; chairman, American Commission for Relief of Belgium, 1915-18; U.S. food administrator, 1917-19; chairman, American Relief Administration, and Russian Relief, 1918-23; chairman, Supreme Economic Conference, 1919; chairman, European Relief Council, 1920; secretary of commerce, 1921-28; thirty-first president, 1929-33; coordinator, European Food Program, 1946; chairman, Committee for Reorganization of the Executive Branch, 1947-49, 1953-55.* **Died:** *October 20, 1964, New York City; buried, West Branch, Iowa.*

*President and Mrs. Hoover with their sons, Herbert, Jr. and Allan and the former's very attractive wife.*

Throughout America the wheels of industry stopped turning. The number of unemployed rose to seventeen million.

Hoover did not believe in federal welfare programs. Such programs should be sponsored by private charities, he felt, and kept on a local level. By the end of his term 5,000 banks had closed their doors. Farm prices were the lowest on record. Business failures exceeded 30,000 a year. The annual gross national income dropped from eighty billion to forty billion. "Prosperity is just around the corner," promised Herbert Hoover. When a Bonus Army of 7,000 veterans descended on Washington in July, 1932, their shacks were burned by Hoover's orders and the petitioners dispersed by force.

In an effort to cope with the depression, Hoover launched the Reconstruction Finance Corporation, to lend federal funds to banks, railways, states and municipalities. But the help provided by the R.F.C. was too little, and it came too late.

When he ran for re-election in 1932 against Franklin Roosevelt, he received 59 electoral votes against 472, or fewer votes than any president campaigning for re-election, except for Taft, had ever received.

Retiring to Palo Alto, California, at the age of 60, Hoover established a research library and museum at Stanford. In 1946, he was appointed by President Truman to coordinate a European relief program. From 1947 to 1949, and from 1953 to 1955, he served on a committee to increase efficiency in the operation of federal agencies. Hoover died in New York on October 20th, 1964, in his 90th year.

*President Hoover throwing out the first ball of the Washington Senators' 1929 baseball season.*

# Franklin D. Roosevelt

**Born:** *January 30, 1882, Hyde Park, New York.*
**Parents:** *James and Sara Delano Roosevelt.*
**Education:** *Harvard, 1904; Columbia Law School, 1907.* **Married:** *1905, Anna Eleanor Roosevelt (1884-1962), six children.* **Career:** *lawyer; author; member, New York state senate, 1911-13; assistant secretary of the navy, 1913-20; governor of New York, 1929-33; thirty-second president, 1933-45.* **Died:** *April 12, 1945, Warm Springs, Georgia; buried, Hyde Park, New York.*

Franklin Delano Roosevelt, an only child, was born on the family farm at Hyde Park, on the banks of the Hudson River 70 miles north of New York City. At the time of his birth, his father was a retired railroad executive, aged 54. His mother, aged 27, was a patrician young lady from New Bedford, Massachusetts. Of early Puritan ancestry, her father had captained his own ships on long voyages to China. Young

Franklin was tutored at home by his mother until he entered Groton. His first playmates had been the children of local farmers and mechanics. As a boy of 10, he was taken by his father to visit President Grover Cleveland who, burdened with the cares of office, patted him on the head and said with a sigh: "My little man, I am going to make a strange wish for you: May you never be president of the United States."

At Harvard, young Roosevelt, now a tall and handsome youth, became editor of *The Crimson,* permanent chairman of his class, and a member of Phi Beta Kappa. Himself a favorite of fortune, he was strongly democratic in his sympathies and campaigned for the election of non-fraternity men to high campus offices. After graduation, he attended law school at Columbia. At 23, he married Eleanor Roosevelt, a distant cousin and an orphaned niece of President Theodore Roosevelt. The President gave away the bride at the brilliant wedding in New York in 1905. A shy, poetic personality, devoted to the quest for social justice, Eleanor Roosevelt shared her husband's career and participated in more far-reaching reform programs than any other president's wife in American history.

While serving as New York state senator, young Roosevelt worked for the nomination and election of Woodrow Wilson in 1912. The next year Wilson appointed him assistant secretary of the navy. The youngest man ever to hold the office, 30-year-old Roosevelt labored with remarkable energy. When America entered World War I, Roosevelt, next to

*The very young Franklin Delano Roosevelt, sitting on his father's shoulder at the age of one year.*

*Roosevelt at Campobello Island with his fiancée, Eleanor Roosevelt, the year before they were married.*

smiling courage, with deepened awareness and sympathy for all human suffering, he continued his fight against the grip of paralysis.

At the urging of friends, who knew his remarkable qualities, Roosevelt stood for governor of New York and was elected in 1928. He launched effective reforms on a state level which won him re-election as governor and a national reputation. In 1932 he was elected president. Entering the White House the year Hitler came into power in Germany, Roosevelt promised "the forgotten man" a "New Deal." In the darkest days of the great depression, he electrified the country, declaring his credo at his inaugural in March, 1933: "First of all, let me assert my firm belief that the only thing we have to fear is fear itself."

As Roosevelt plunged into action, Congress voted him the broadest emergency powers ever accorded a president in time of peace. In the next hundred days, working unceasingly with his advisers, a dedicated group of social scientists known as the "Brain Trust," Roosevelt launched the boldest reform program in American history.

During his first term he set up huge public works to start the wheels of industry rolling again. He found work for the jobless, food for the hungry, shelter for the homeless. He established scores of federal agencies. The Civilian Conservation Corps employed three million jobless youths to help conserve the country's natural resources. The Works Progress Administration employed ten million men to build new roads and

Wilson, was the most active man in government. Cutting through red tape to expedite preparations, he broke enough laws, he remarked later, to send him to jail for 999 years. He attended the peace conference at Versailles in 1919 and witnessed Woodrow Wilson's heroic efforts to launch the League of Nations. Wilson and Jefferson had perhaps the deepest influence on Roosevelt's political philosophy.

At the Democratic Convention in San Francisco in 1920, Roosevelt was nominated vice-president. The country, eager to return to "normalcy," elected the Harding-Coolidge ticket. Roosevelt returned to New York, intending to resume his law practice.

The following summer he vacationed with his family at Campobello Island, in New Brunswick on the Atlantic coast. It was here that he was stricken with polio and paralyzed from the waist down. There was no known cure for the crippling disease. At 40, he was considered a permanent invalid, doomed to an early death.

But Roosevelt fought the faceless enemy. He found a small run-down resort in Warm Springs, Georgia, where the waters seemed to have a curative effect on his legs. He bought the resort and set up a non-profit clinic to help other sufferers. For three years he exercised his afflicted muscles. In 1924, he was able to stand from his wheel chair; with the help of iron braces and a cane he could take a few steps. With

*Roosevelt paddling his Indian canoe at Campobello. This was 14 years before he was stricken with polio.*

*The Roosevelt family on Christmas Day, 1932.*
*Seated at the then-Governer's left is his mother, Mrs.*
*Sara Delano Roosevelt; at his right, his wife.*

bridges, schools and hospitals, and other public buildings in hundreds of towns throughout the country. It included nearly four hundred federal projects for artists, writers, musicians, and actors. The National Youth Administration found part-time jobs for students. The Farm Security Administration helped millions of farmers. Agencies were set up to regulate the stock market, to lend billions of dollars to businessmen. The Tennessee Valley Authority built a chain of giant dams, to bring cheap water, power, and light to seven states in the South.

In 1936, Roosevelt was re-elected by the unprecedented electoral vote of 523 to 8, losing only two states, Maine and Vermont. During his second term, Roosevelt met with increasing hostility from big business interests whose power he threatened and who now accused him of giving labor too much power. "They are unanimous in their hate for me," said Roosevelt, "and I welcome their hate....Some of these people really forget how sick they were....But I know how the knees of all of our rugged individualists were trembling four years ago and how their hearts fluttered. Washington did not look like a dangerous bureaucracy to them, then. It looked like an emergency hospital...." Denounced as a traitor to his class, "That Man in the White House" became the chief target of conservative abuse.

The most vigorous opposition to Roosevelt's reforms came from the Supreme Court. In only two years they issued nearly 1600 injunctions striking down congressional acts they considered unconstitutional. Roosevelt angrily attacked the "nine old men"

*President Roosevelt with Prime Minister Churchill at the Casablanca Conference in January of 1943.*

*While in Egypt in November of 1943, President Roosevelt conferred with Ibn Saud, the king of Saudi Arabia.*

with a proposal to appoint seven additional judges of his own choice. Congress sharply refused to pass this "court packing" legislation.

With Europe ablaze with Hitler's wars of aggression, Roosevelt tried to alert America. He was attacked as a warmonger by the isolationists. Finally, in March, 1941, Congress passed the Lend-Lease Act, which empowered Roosevelt to send supplies to Great Britian, Russia, and other countries whose defense he considered vital to the safety of the United States.

On December 7, 1941, "a day that will live in infamy," Pearl Harbor was attacked by Japan, Hitler's Asiatic partner, in a surprise raid by air and by submarine which destroyed an important part of the U. S. fleet. America's vast resources were mobilized. The whole country stood behind Roosevelt who now, in alliance with British and Russian leaders, conducted the global war against the Axis powers of Germany, Italy, and Japan.

As Woodrow Wilson had stated the objectives of democracy in his Fourteen Points, so Roosevelt declared his program of the Four Freedoms:

"In future days, which we seek to make secure, we look forward to a world founded upon four essential freedoms.

"The first is freedom of speech and expression—everywhere in the world.

"The second is freedom of every person to worship God in his own way—everywhere in the world.

"The third is freedom from want—which, translated into world terms, means economic understandings which will secure every nation a healthy peacetime life for its inhabitants—everywhere in the world.

"The fourth is freedom from fear—which, translated into world terms, means a world-wide reduction of armaments to such a point and in such a thorough fashion that no nation will be in a position to commit an act of physical aggression against any neighbor—anywhere in the world."

Roosevelt looked to the United Nations as the organization that would realize the Four Freedoms program. In February, 1945, he attended a meeting at Yalta with Prime Minister Churchill and the dictator of Russia, Joseph Stalin. Roosevelt believed that the Big Three could cooperate and establish the conditions for a durable world peace. On April 12, 1945, exhausted by his long labors in safely guiding the country through the worst depression and most destructive war in history, he died at Warm Springs, Georgia.

The world was stunned by his death. A tower of strength had fallen, and nations went into mourning. Flags were at half-mast in the capitals of Europe, schools were closed, and parliaments adjourned. Men in the street spoke their grief in all languages. Winston Churchill called him, "The greatest champion of freedom who ever brought help and comfort from the New World to the Old."

91

# Harry S. Truman

**Born:** *May 8, 1884, Lamar, Missouri.* **Parents:** *John Anderson and Martha Ellen Young Truman.* **Education:** *high school.* **Married:** *1919, Elizabeth (Bess) Virginia Wallace (1885-    ), one child.* **Career:** *farmer; artillery officer, World War I; store owner; judge, Jackson County, Missouri, court, 1922-24; presiding judge, 1926-34; U.S. senator, 1935-45; vice-president, January 20 to April 12, 1945; thirty-third president, 1945-53.* **Died:** *December 26, 1972, Kansas City, Missouri; buried, Independence, Missouri.*

"Last night the whole weight of the moon and the stars fell on me," he told reporters on April 13, 1945. "I've got the most awful responsibility a man ever had. If you fellows ever pray, pray for me." Within four hours after Roosevelt's death, Harry S. Truman had taken the oath of office. He was the seventh man to step into the presidency through the accident of death.

Son of a horse and mule trader, Truman was born on a farm near Lamar, Missouri. While attending high school in Independence he worked in the local drug store as window washer and floor scrubber. At 17, he applied for a cadetship to West Point but was turned down because of his defective vision. Before he was 21 he held temporary jobs as timekeeper on a railroad gang and bookkeeper for a Kansas City bank. From the age of 22 to 33 he worked as a dirt farmer on the family farm. In 1917, a member of the National Guard, he attended field artillery school at Fort Sill in Oklahoma; in April, 1918, he was sent overseas as a lieutenant. He saw action at St.-Mihiel and the Meuse-Argonne. A member of his company recorded that "he was one of the fastest calculators of artillery data in the whole division."

After the war, in partnership with one of his sergeants, he opened a men's clothing store in Kansas City. When the business went bankrupt in 1922, Truman took upon himself to pay off the creditors; in time he did so in full. Through the sponsorship of Tom Pendergast, boss of the Missouri Democratic political machine, he was elected judge and county official in Jackson County. Though Pendergast was later sent to jail for income tax evasion, Truman himself retained an unblemished record as an honest public servant.

In 1934, he was elected U. S. senator; in 1940, he was re-elected. In the Senate he served as chairman of a watch-dog committee on defense expenditures. His efficiency in safeguarding the people's interest saved millions of dollars on defense contracts. Shortly before the Democratic convention of 1944, President Roosevelt expressed a preference for William O. Douglas or Harry Truman as his running mate. Though Truman went to the convention to nominate his friend James Byrnes for vice-president, Truman himself was nominated. Three months after Roosevelt's fourth inaugural, Truman was president of the United States.

Aware of his own limitations and conscious of the unflattering comparisons made between himself and his great predecessor, Truman made little effort to be anything but himself, an average man whom chance and the democratic process had cast into the presidency in a time of world upheavals. In general, he tried to carry on Roosevelt's policies.

In 1945, Truman had to make one of the most agonizing decisions ever made by a president. "It was my responsibility as president," he wrote later, "to force the Japanese war lords to come to terms as quickly as possible with the minimum loss of lives. I then made my final decision. And that final decision was mine alone to make." On August 6, 1945, on Truman's orders, an army plane flew over Hiroshima and dropped an atom bomb which killed 78,000 Japanese in one blast. On August 9, a second bomb was dropped over Nagasaki, killing 74,000. "Almost immediately after the dropping of the second bomb, the Japanese surrendered," wrote Truman.

The public opinion polls, most of the press and radio, and even his own party predicted Truman's defeat in the presidential race of 1948. But Truman conducted a vigorous "whistle-stop" campaign. He traveled some 30,000 miles to deliver 350 speeches in a "Give 'em Hell" campaign against the "do-nothing" 80th Congress which had obstructed his domestic and foreign program. In the biggest election upset on record, Truman was returned to the White House. He did not receive the majority of the popular vote, but he won a plurality of over two million votes and an electoral vote of 303 against 189 for Thomas E. Dewey, the Republican candidate.

Hampered again by a divided Congress, Truman continued his policy of furnishing economic and technical aid to countries throughout the world through the Marshall Plan, the Truman Doctrine, the Point Four Program. He sought to contain the spread of communism in the Cold War with Soviet Russia by

*Below: Truman with Prime Minister Attlee, Marshal Stalin, and their advisers at the Potsdam Conference.*

*Above: The* Chicago Tribune *was so sure Dewey would win in 1948 that it said so in the early editions.*

*The Trumans with their daughter, Margaret, in Key West, Florida, after the hard-fought and successful 1948 campaign.*

forming military alliances with western Europe. In 1950 he sent American troops into Korea, under United Nations auspices, in an attempt to halt Communist aggression. The war dragged on until a cease-fire was negotiated in 1954.

Truman retired to his home in Independence, Missouri, in 1953, as vigorous at 68 as when he assumed the presidency. Before his death in his 88th year, he wrote his two-volume memoirs, *Years of Decisions* and *Years of Trial and Hope*.

*President Truman speaking at ceremonies honoring the signing of the Atlantic Pact in April of 1949.*

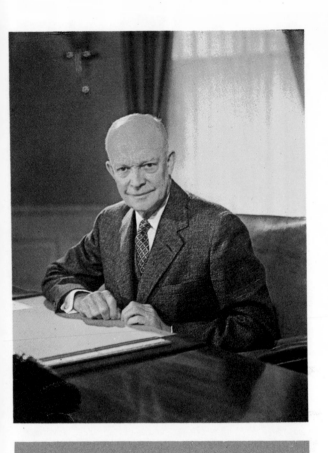

in a covered wagon. His father worked as a mechanic in railroad shops in Texas. Imbued with the teachings of the Bible, his parents raised six sturdy sons, each of whom made notable contributions to society.

At Abilene High School, the future president was best in baseball and football, although a class prophet predicted that "Ike will wind up as a professor of history." To save money for college, he worked in a dairy, 84 hours a week. At West Point he made the football team and played against the noted athlete Jim Thorpe. Graduating as 2nd lieutenant in 1915, he served in the army and slowly advanced in rank during the next three decades. In 1941, he was a colonel, serving on General Douglas MacArthur's staff in the Philippines. During these years he gained recognition as a planner and strategist. In 1942, General George C. Marshall put him in command of the Allied invasion of North Africa. In 1943 "General Ike" became Supreme Allied Commander.

Hero of the crusade in Europe, he returned home in 1945 to find himself more popular than any Ameri-

*Lieutenant Dwight Eisenhower and his bride after their marriage in Denver on July 1, 1916.*

# Dwight D. Eisenhower

**Born:** *October 14, 1890, Denison, Texas.* **Parents:** *David Jacob and Ida Elizabeth Stoever Eisenhower.* **Education:** *West Point, 1915.* **Married:** *1916, Mary (Mamie) Geneva Doud (1896- ), two children.* **Career:** *U.S. Army, 1915-52; supreme commander, Allied Expeditionary Forces, 1943-45; Chief of Staff, 1945-48; president, Columbia University, 1948-53; supreme commander, NATO, 1950-52; thirty-fourth president, 1953-61. Rank as general of the army restored, 1961.* **Died:** *March 29, 1969, Washington, D.C.; buried, Abilene, Kansas.*

Dwight David Eisenhower was raised in Abilene, Kansas, at the end of the Chisholm Trail. His ancestors were devout Mennonites who had fled from Germany to Pennsylvania in the early 18th century to escape religious persecution. His grandfather, Jacob Eisenhower, a farmer and preacher, moved to Kansas

*General Eisenhower in Frankfurt, Germany, after the signing of the German surrender in 1945. With him are (left) Field Marshal Montgomery and (right) Soviet Marshal Zhukov and Air Chief Marshal Sir Arthur Tedder.*

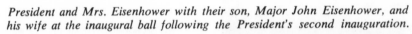

*President and Mrs. Eisenhower with their son, Major John Eisenhower, and his wife at the inaugural ball following the President's second inauguration.*

can general since U. S. Grant. During his tour of the country, millions through the land shouted themselves hoarse, calling "Ike, Ike, Ike!" Removing his uniform as a five-star general, Eisenhower became president of Columbia University in 1948. In 1950, he was appointed Supreme Commander of the NATO forces in Europe.

Though both the Democratic and Republican parties sought him as their candidate, he did not believe that "a full-time professional soldier" should hold the presidency. Twice he refused to run.

Drafted by the Republicans in 1952, he was elected president by the largest popular vote in the nation's history, receiving 33,936,234 votes to 27,314,992 votes for Adlai E. Stevenson, the Democratic candidate. Running for re-election in 1956, Eisenhower won an even larger popular vote, receiving 35,581,003 votes to 26,031,322 for Stevenson, with an electoral vote of 457 to 74. His personal popularity was responsible for the triumph; the Republican party itself won only a scanty majority in Congress.

As president, Eisenhower followed a middle-of-the-road course. He called himself a moderate and advocated "dynamic conservatism." He tried to revitalize his party in the form of a "New Republicanism." He favored foreign aid and disarmament and negotiating for peace from a position of strength. He proposed an "Atoms for Peace" program for the development of atomic energy on a world-wide basis.

In an age of anxiety, the first decade of the Cold War, President Eisenhower did what he could to strengthen America's defenses. "Only strength can cooperate," he said. "Weakness cannot cooperate: it can only beg."

A soldier who fought for peace, a victorious commander without political ambitions, a man who twice refused to run for the presidency, Eisenhower left the White House in January, 1961, at the age of 70, the oldest man ever to have held the office. He retired to his farm at Gettysburg, Pennsylvania. He died on March 29, 1969, at Walter Reed General Hospital in Washington, D.C., and was buried at Abilene, Kansas.

*Ex-President Eisenhower and his wife at their farm at Gettysburg, Pennsylvania, on his 72nd birthday.*

© Fabian Bachrach

# John F. Kennedy

**Born:** *May 29, 1917, Brookline, Massachusetts.*
**Parents:** *Joseph Patrick and Rose Fitzgerald Kennedy.* **Education:** *Harvard, 1940.* **Married:** *1953, Jacqueline Lee Bouvier (1929-    ), three children.* **Career:** *author, naval officer, 1941-45; newspaper correspondent; U.S. representative from Massachusetts, 1947-53; U.S. senator, 1953-61; thirty-fifth president, 1961-63.* **Died:** *November 22, 1963, Dallas, Texas; buried, Arlington, Virginia.*

John Fitzgerald Kennedy's background is part of the American saga. Benjamin Franklin saw the first boatload of immigrants from Ireland arrive in the port of Boston. They came as indentured servants who had bound themselves for five or six years in exchange for passage to America. The spirited sons of the Irish became leaders of the Revolution, furnishing more than

half the men and officers in Washington's army. Kennedy's great-grandfather emerged from the slums of Boston where Irish Catholics had suffered social and economic discrimination, as indicated by the once-familiar newspaper notice, "Only Protestants Need Apply." His paternal grandfather, Patrick J. Kennedy, served in both houses of the Massachusetts legislature. His maternal grandfather, John F. Fitzgerald, was mayor of Boston at the turn of the century.

His father, Joseph P. Kennedy, a dynamic and colorful individualist, embarked on a variety of ventures, including shipbuilding, movie-making, real estate, and banking. He built up one of the largest fortunes in America. Though a multimillionaire, he was also a staunch and outspoken New Dealer. Under President Roosevelt he held several posts, including that of ambassador to Britain from 1937 to 1941.

Second eldest of nine children, John F. Kennedy was a member of a closely knit, affectionate, yet highly competitive family. He attended the Choate School in Connecticut before going on to Harvard. There young Kennedy went out for varsity football and the swimming team. He was somewhat overshadowed by his brother, Joseph, Jr., who was more popular as an athlete and more brilliant as a student.

Graduating from Harvard *cum laude* in 1940 with a bachelor of science degree, Kennedy did graduate work in economics at Stanford University. The following year came Pearl Harbor. At 24, Kennedy entered the Navy, served as a PT boat commander, and saw extensive action in the South Pacific. In one dramatic action in the Solomon Islands he was severely wounded and nearly lost his life.

The action took place on August 2, 1943, shortly after midnight, when a Japanese destroyer attacked

*The Kennedy family in England in 1937, when Joseph Kennedy was ambassador there. John is at the far left.*

Lt. Kennedy's patrol boat, bearing down on it at 30 knots and cutting it in two. The broken hull burst into flames that lit up the dark waters. Two men were killed. Kennedy and his surviving crew of ten kept afloat in a sea of gasoline by clinging to a part of the burning hull. Towing one man, Kennedy swam five hours to reach a coral island behind the enemy lines. Nine days of thirst and starvation followed. At the base, the men were given up for lost.

Kennedy and the other survivors continued to struggle till they reached an island with natives. Kennedy carved a message into the shell of a coconut: "ELEVEN ALIVE, NATIVE KNOWS POSIT AND REEFS, NAURU ISLAND. KENNEDY." He gave it to an islander who then paddled off in his canoe to alert the New Zealand patrol. Next day a rescue party arrived to save the 11 half-dead survivors.

Awarded the Purple Heart and the Navy and Marine Corps medal, Kennedy was cited by Admiral William Halsey for "his courage, endurance, and excellent leadership." He was retired from active duty in March, 1944, because of the spinal injury he received in the Solomons. In August of the same year, his brother Joe was killed while piloting a plane on a mission over Belgium.

As correspondent for the International News Service in 1945, Kennedy covered the United Nations Conference in San Francisco. In 1946, at the age of 29, he entered the political arena, running for Congress as representative of the 11th Congressional District of Massachusetts. In 1952, he started his strenuous campaign against Senator Henry Cabot Lodge, whose re-election was considered certain. Kennedy defeated Lodge by 70,000 votes and became the third Democrat ever to be elected to the Senate from Massachusetts.

While serving in the House, he attended a dinner party in Washington where he met a 22-year-old beauty, Jacqueline Lee Bouvier. A student at George Washington University, she had studied at Vassar and at the Sorbonne. They married at Newport, Rhode Island, in 1953.

In 1956, Kennedy published *Profiles in Courage*, a study of notable non-conformists in American history. The book received the Pulitzer Prize.

In January, 1960, before the national convention, Senator Kennedy pursued the difficult course of entering seven state primaries, and won all seven. After his nomination, he continued his vigorous campaign, an unusual feature of which was his four television debates with Vice-President Richard Nixon. Never before had rival candidates been heard and seen by an audience estimated at seventy million.

The debates did much to make Kennedy a nationally popular figure. On November 8, 1960, he was elected president, polling 34,227,096 votes out of a total of almost sixty-nine million.

*President and Mrs. Kennedy with their children at Palm Beach, Easter, 1963. A third child died later that year.*

The youngest man ever elected to the presidency, the first Catholic, and the first president born in the twentieth century, Kennedy stated his creed in his eloquent inaugural address in which he summoned his countrymen to join "a struggle against the common enemies of man: tyranny, poverty, disease and war itself . . ."

In the two years and ten months of his administration, President Kennedy gave new style and vigor to his office. He sponsored the Peace Corps, a space project to explore the moon, a plan to save the Nile monuments. His handling of the Cuban missile crisis has been called "a textbook classic in modern diplomacy." His chief accomplishment was perhaps the Test Ban Treaty, a major step in reducing the hazard from nuclear weapons and the arms race. "We shall not regret our commitment to the cause of man's survival," he said, signing the treaty on October 7, 1963.

Six weeks later, in an act which shocked and horrified the world, he was assassinated by a sniper in Dallas, Texas—on Friday, November 22, 1963, at 12:30 P.M. President Kennedy's funeral on November 25, followed by a vast procession of mourners, was attended by some 220 foreign chiefs of state. Winston Churchill said: "The loss to the United States and to the world is incalculable."

# Lyndon B. Johnson

**Born:** *August 27, 1908, near Stonewall, Texas.*
**Parents:** *Samuel Ealy and Rebekah Baines Johnson.* **Education:** *Southwest State Teachers College, San Marcos, Texas, 1930; Georgetown University Law School.* **Married:** *1934, Claudia Alta (Lady Bird) Taylor (1912-    ), two children.*
**Career:** *teacher; congressional secretary, 1932-35; Texas state director, National Youth Administration, 1935-37; U.S. representative, 1937-49; commander, U.S.N.R., on active duty, 1941-42; U.S. senator, 1949-61; vice-president, 1961-63; thirty-sixth president, 1963-1969.* **Died:** *January 22, 1973, at the "L.B.J." ranch near Johnson City, Texas.*

As vice-president, Lyndon Baines Johnson had accompanied Kennedy on his fatal tour of Texas. On November 22, 1963, less than two hours after Kennedy was officially pronounced dead, Johnson took his oath of office as President of the United States.

The ceremony took place aboard the plane that brought the widowed Jacqueline Kennedy and the late President's body back to Washington. Five days later President Johnson addressed Congress: "The greatest leader of our time has been struck down by the foulest deed of our time...No words are strong enough to express our determination to continue the forward thrust of America that he began."

With this promise Johnson launched his administration. At 55, he was a master of practical politics and had behind him thirty years' experience in the legislative arena. Vigorous and persuasive, he had a record of success and was highly influential in Congress.

His education in the school of democracy began in the pioneer West. "I was born to the hill country of Texas," he said. "A remote region then, still remote today." It was a country of little ranches in the arid hills of southwest Texas. His birthplace was a crossroads village near Johnson City, a frontier outpost founded by his grandfather. Graduating from the Johnson City High School, at 16 he was a stringy black-haired youth, six feet tall, "too thin to throw a shadow at noon." In search of employment, he hitchhiked to California and did odd jobs for a few months as a car washer, an elevator operator, a handyman in a cafe. Returning home, he worked on a road gang and drove a truck. He then entered State Teachers

*Then-Senator and Mrs. Johnson photographed at their ranch in 1960. The ranch is named the "L. B. J."*

College at San Marcos and, earning his way, graduated in 1930. At 23, he was a teacher of public speaking and debating in a Houston high school.

He started his political apprenticeship in Washington at 24 as secretary to Richard Kleberg, U.S. representative from Texas. Two years later he met Claudia Taylor, nicknamed Lady Bird, a graduate of the University of Texas; after a whirlwind six weeks' courtship, they were married in 1934.

Johnson's active support of the New Deal won President Roosevelt's notice and led to his appointment as Texas director of the National Youth Administration in 1935. Two years later he resigned to run for Congress. Energetic and ambitious, he was elected and re-elected, term after term, for the next 24 years. In 1941, he volunteered for active duty in the Navy three days after Pearl Harbor; serving as a lieutenant-commander, he flew on a mission over New Guinea, won the Silver Star for gallantry in action, then returned to Congress in 1942. At 44, he was the Democratic leader in the Senate, the youngest man ever to hold that post. A champion of civil rights, he led the move in 1954 to censure Senator Joseph McCarthy. "No demagogue is going to lead the people into the path of bigotry," said Johnson. He became John F. Kennedy's choice for vice-president in 1960 and served as such until Kennedy's death in 1963.

Running against Barry Goldwater in 1964, with Hubert Humphrey as his mate, Johnson was elected with 43 million popular votes, or 15 million votes more than those obtained by Goldwater. Backed by the largest popular vote ever cast for any presidential candidate, Johnson announced his program to build the Great Society. "I am resolved that we shall win the tomorrows before us, that we shall move toward a new American greatness," he declared.

But although he got important legislation through Congress, including Medicare (proposed by President Kennedy) and measures affecting education, civil rights and the fight against poverty, Johnson soon became a center of national controversy and division. This was due largely to his conduct of the war in Vietnam, which he had escalated from time to time in pursuit of a decisive victory. Both his program and his prestige suffered drastic damage. The prolonged and costly war to contain communism in Southeast Asia was opposed by a growing number of Americans who considered it unjustifiable to waste American lives and resources in Asia at the expense of social reforms which were needed at home. Reflecting tensions in the ghettoes, waves of civil disorders swept the country. The year 1968 witnessed the assassination of Martin Luther King, Jr., in Memphis and of Robert F. Kennedy in Los Angeles; it saw bloody riots in Washington, Chicago, and other cities. Before the end of his term, Lyndon Johnson had become less popular perhaps than any president since Andrew Johnson, who was impeached in March, 1868.

In March, 1968, Johnson broadcast his decision not to run again: by taking himself out of the presidential race, he hoped to reduce the tensions and divisions which had split the country. In November, as a way of furthering the peace negotiations in Paris, he suspended the bombing of North Vietnam. He left the White House in January, 1969, returned to Texas to write his memoirs, and died on his ranch in 1973.

*On a trip to California President Johnson bids goodbye to a group of U.S. Marines bound for the war in Vietnam.*

# Richard M. Nixon

**Born:** *January 9, 1913, Yorba Linda, California.*
**Parents:** *Francis A. and Hannah Milhous Nixon.*
**Education:** *Whittier College, 1934; Duke University Law School, 1937.* **Married:** *1940, Thelma (Pat) Ryan (1912-    ), two daughters.* **Career:** *Lawyer, naval officer, 1937-1945; U.S. representative from California, 1946-50; U.S. senator, 1950-52; vice-president, 1952-60; thirty-seventh president 1969-1974, resigned August 9, 1974.*

Born on a lemon farm in Yorba Linda on the outskirts of Los Angeles, Richard Nixon was the second son of poor but deeply pious Quaker parents. As a boy, he attended church four times every Sunday; his father taught Sunday school; his mother prayed that Richard

would become a preacher. Both his Quaker great-grandmother and great-great-grandmother had been noted itinerant preachers.

Nixon's paternal and maternal forebears came from Ireland and settled in Delaware before the American Revolution. When the first public reading of the Declaration of Independence took place—in Philadelphia, on July 8, 1776—the man who read it to the crowd in front of the State House was Colonel John Nixon. On Christmas Eve of the same fateful year, another Nixon crossed the Delaware River with General George Washington.

When Richard was nine, his family moved some thirteen miles to the town of Whittier (founded by Quakers), where his father ran a grocery store and gas station with the help of his wife and four sons. "Our family was poor," Richard Nixon recalled, "but we never thought of ourselves as poor. We always had enough to eat...In grammar school I was dressed mostly in hand-me-downs. Once in a while we'd go to a movie. But that was a luxury...There was illness in the family. We all worked like hell. We had to. There was a drive to succeed, to survive almost...My father was a very competitive man. He loved to argue with anybody about anything. I guess I acquired my competitive instinct from him."

In Whittier High School young Nixon emerged as the best student in his class and the champion boy debater of southern California. "He could take any side and win," his debating coach said. At the Quaker college of Whittier, among five hundred students, he was again the champion debater, second in his class and president of the student body. He went in for dramatics and football, his favorite sport, although, in the words of a classmate, "he just wasn't meant to be a football player." But his football coach remembered: "There was one thing about Nixon. He played every scrimmage as though the championship were at stake."

At 21, Richard Nixon entered the Duke University Law School on a scholarship. "Like most of us, Dick had an N.Y.A. [National Youth Administration] job to keep the depression wolf from the door," one student recalled. "I had the impression that Nixon was extremely poor. I don't think he ever ate more than two meals a day while I knew him in law school..." Considered shy and aloof, Nixon was nicknamed Gloomy Gus, after a cartoon character. His only known escapade had a serious aim: he crawled through the transom of the dean's office to check the records for his scholastic rating. He stood third in his class of about one hundred, and became its president in his senior year.

Returning in 1937 to practice law in Whittier, he met Pat Ryan at a Little Theater tryout, and immediately proposed to her. Three years later they were married. After Pearl Harbor, Nixon entered the Navy as a junior officer and served in the Pacific until the end of 1945. Then, at the invitation of a Republican group in Whittier, he entered his first race for Congress, running against a popular Democratic incumbent. In a series of five debates, Nixon challenged his opponent as being soft on communism, and won his seat in the House. Thereafter, he made anti-communism a leading issue in his campaigns.

He gained national attention in 1948 through the sensational Hiss-Chambers espionage case, which Nixon investigated as a member of the House Committee on Un-American Activities. In his book, *Six Crises*, Nixon places this stormy drama as the first great crisis in his career. In 1950, in another anti-communist campaign, he won a seat in the Senate. In the presidential campaign of 1952, as Eisenhower's running mate, Nixon was accused of accepting a secret fund from a "millionaires' club." In danger of being dumped by his party, Senator Nixon faced the nation on television with his dog Checkers and, in a dramatic broadcast, vindicated himself. At 39 he became the second youngest vice-president in U.S. history.

As President Eisenhower's personal envoy, he went on goodwill missions to fifty-six countries on five continents. On a South American tour in 1958, he was attacked by angry crowds of anti-American students and narrowly escaped with his life. In 1959, while visiting Moscow, he made headlines by a sharp, finger-jabbing "kitchen debate" with Soviet premier Khrushchev.

Running for the presidency in 1960, the great debater was ironically the loser in four television debates with an underdog rival, John F. Kennedy, who won the election by a hairline margin. Two years later, Nixon lost his bid for governorship of his native state

by 300,000 votes. In a bitter speech to the press, he appeared to renounce his political ambitions. He left California and joined a law firm in New York. For seven years he held no public office.

Then, in the political and social chaos of 1968, Nixon staged a surprising comeback. Launching a well-organized campaign for the presidency, he won a close race against Vice-President Hubert Humphrey. He promised to end the fighting in Vietnam, advocated an all-volunteer army to replace the draft, and proposed "black capitalism"—in effect, a Marshall Plan for Black America.

Shortly after he took his oath of office, President Nixon ordered the secret bombings of Cambodia. The bombings continued for 14 months, without the consent of Congress and without destroying resistance in Vietnam. The "Pentagon Papers," leaked in 1971 and published by *The New York Times* and *The Washington Post,* revealed that the American people had been misled about U.S. actions in Vietnam. President Nixon had reduced the number of U.S. troops but increased U.S. air and naval forces in a grim and deadly effort to crush resistance and hopefully produce long-range peace in Asia. Finally, in March, 1973, the last U.S. troops left Vietnam, after cease-fire orders terminated the long fiasco. The war in the jungles of Southeast Asia proved to be the longest, costliest, and perhaps most futile war in U.S. history.

In 1972, an election year, President Nixon made a spectacular about-face to end the cold war with China and Russia. After some 20 years of non-recognition, Communist China, containing about one-fourth of the earth's population, was admitted into the United Nations late in 1971. In February, 1972, President Nixon flew to Peking to confer with the leaders of

*Touring South America as Vice-President in 1958, Nixon exchanges words with anti-U.S. students in Lima, Peru.*

*President Nixon speaks to the nation about the Watergate scandal from his office in Washington, D.C., April 30, 1974.*

Communist China and foster friendly relations. Three months later, he flew to Moscow for a summit meeting with Premier Brezhnev, in an effort to limit the production and use of atomic weapons, to encourage detente and develop trade with Soviet Russia.

The domestic scene was not so encouraging, though. During the presidential race of 1972, the police in Washington arrested five men who had burglarized the Democratic National Committee's offices in the Watergate Hotel and had installed wiretapping devices to spy out information that might prove damaging to political opponents. At the time, President Nixon assured the press: "There is no involvement by the White House in the Watergate affair." He was re-elected by a landslide vote over his opponent, Senator George McGovern of South Dakota.

At his glittering inaugural party in January, 1973, he promised the country a new era of peace and prosperity. But within the next six months, the Senate committee investigating the Watergate affair uncovered a network of corruption in government which threatened to overshadow the Teapot Dome scandals of the Harding administration. The televised hearings were seen and heard by 100 million Americans.

The testimony implicated, in bribery, fraud, and obstruction of justice, three members of Nixon's cabinet, his two chief White House aides, and scores of officials. A number of them were convicted and sent to prison. Vice-President Spiro Agnew resigned, accepting conviction for income tax evasion, to avoid prosecution for bribery. President Nixon himself maintained his innocence. For more than a year he refused to release to Congress the White House tapes relating to Watergate. When finally released in August, 1974, the tapes implicated that he had tampered with justice in 1972. Other evidence revealed misuse of the FBI, the CIA, and the IRS. Talk of impeachment spread throughout the country.

In view of the new evidence, Republican leaders called on him to advise him they could not prevent his impeachment and conviction for violating his oath of office, for obstructing justice, and for defying Congress. On August 9, 1974, faced with the worst crisis in his crisis-ridden career, President Nixon chose to resign. Bidding farewell to the White House, he retired to his estate in San Clemente and prepared to write his memoirs, to present his own case, in an effort to vindicate his conduct.

# Gerald R. Ford

**Born:** *July 14, 1913, Omaha, Nebraska.* **Parents:** *Leslie Lynch King and Dorothy Gardner King; adopted by stepfather, Gerald Rudolph Ford, in 1916.* **Education:** *University of Michigan, 1935; Yale University Law School, 1941.* **Married:** *1948, Elizabeth Bloomer Warren (1917-    ), three sons, one daughter.* **Career:** *coach, lawyer, naval officer; U.S. representative, 1948-73; vice-president, 1973-74; thirty-eighth president, 1974-77.*

"Our long national nightmare is over," President Ford declared in the East Room of the White House after taking his oath of office. "As we bind up the internal wounds of Watergate, let brotherly love purge our hearts of suspicion and hate..."

A conservative Republican from the Middle West, known for his integrity, he was acclaimed and applauded by more than 90 per cent of the country. But less than a month after his elevation to the highest office, his popularity suffered a decline.

Born in Nebraska, he was named Leslie Lynch King, Jr., after his father, a wool trader in Omaha. His parents were divorced when he was two, and his mother returned with him to her parents' home in Grand Rapids, Michigan. Soon afterwards, she married a paint salesman, Gerald Rudolph Ford, who adopted the boy and renamed him after himself.

At South High School in Grand Rapids, the future president proved an outstanding football player: in his senior year he was star center on the team that won the state championship. Entering the University of Michigan on an athletic scholarship, he made the collegiate All-America team in 1935 and, after graduation, received offers from professional football teams. Turning down the offers, he enrolled at Yale, where he coached both football and freshman boxing to help defray his expenses in law school. In 1941, Jerry Ford received his law degree from Yale, graduating in the upper third of his class, then returned to Grand Rapids to start his law practice.

His career as a lawyer was interrupted by World War II. Commissioned as an ensign, he entered the Navy in 1942. For a year he coached aviation cadets at Chapel Hill, North Carolina. Then, volunteering for sea duty, he served aboard the aircraft carrier *USS Monterey* in the South Pacific. Known as a dependable "team player," he was discharged in 1946 with the rank of lieutenant commander.

Returning to Grand Rapids, he became active in local politics. At the age of 35, he ran for Congress. Defeating the incumbent, a four-term isolationist congressman, Ford was elected representative from Michigan's 5th District. Shortly after his election, he married Mrs. Elizabeth Bloomer Warren, a 30-year-old divorcée who had danced with the Martha Graham dance troupe.

During the next quarter of a century (1948-73), Congressman Ford was re-elected 12 times. In Congress, always a loyal team player, he followed the Republican party line. He described himself as "a moderate on domestic issues, a conservative in fiscal affairs, and a dyed-in-the-wool internationalist in foreign affairs."

In October, 1973, after Vice-President Spiro Agnew's resignation, Nixon nominated Ford for the office, under Amendment 25, a recent amendment to the Constitution. During the next eight months, Vice-President Ford traveled widely, making more than 500 appearances to defend Nixon's record on Watergate. On August 9, 1974, the day after Nixon's resignation, Ford became President. He promised

*President Ford discusses international affairs with Secretary of State Henry Kissinger.*

"openness and candor" in his administration, and the country turned to him with hope and relief. A month later, without consulting Congress, he granted Nixon "a full, complete and absolute pardon" for all the crimes he may have committed. As a result, President Ford's popularity plummeted.

In the spring of 1975, he made urgent appeals to Congress for fresh aid to South Vietnam and Cambodia, both on the verge of surrendering to the communist forces; but Congress, opposed to further involvement, refused his appeals. During 1975, America was suffering from the effects of a world-wide recession, spiraling inflation, the highest unemploy-

ment rate since the Great Depression, and a severe energy crisis. The last was caused in part by the Arab countries' decision to raise the price of their oil, in retaliation for U.S. support of Israel. As a remedy for the ever-mounting inflation, Ford urged consumers to buy less.

To add to his problems, in September, 1975, two separate assassination attempts were made against him in California. Both would-be assassins were women; both tried to shoot the President; and both were frustrated.

During his administration, President Ford continued Nixon's policies of detente with Soviet Russia and accommodation with the People's Republic of China. He attended summit meetings in Vladivostock and Helsinki, to limit the atomic arms race. He met with Chinese leaders in Peking. He announced the "Pacific Doctrine" of peace for all, and hostility toward none.

In the election year of 1976, Ford's policies and performance were sharply attacked by Ronald Reagan, a fellow Republican and an avid contender for the presidency. After winning a close primary race against Reagan, President Ford turned to face an uphill battle against his next opponent, Democrat James Carter from Georgia. Stressing the fact that the U.S. was at "peace with freedom" in the Bicentennial year of 1976, Ford reminded people that the country was well respected around the globe as the leader of the free world, and that the recession of 1975 was diminishing slowly due to his solid, steady domestic policy of low spending and income tax reductions. Debating Jimmy Carter three times on national television, Ford slowly gained ground but still lost a close election in November, 1976.

*President Ford shaking hands and campaigning hard in an effort to gain an edge in the close 1976 election.*

# James E. Carter

**Born:** *October 1, 1924, Plains, Georgia.* **Parents:** *James Earl and Lillian Gordy Carter.* **Education:** *Georgia Southwestern Junior College, 1942; Georgia Institute of Technology, 1943; U.S. Naval Academy, 1947; Union College, 1952.* **Married:** *1946, Rosalynn Smith; three sons, one daughter.* **Career:** *U.S. Navy officer, 1947-53; peanut farmer, 1953-70; senator, Georgia state legislature, 1962-66; governor of Georgia, 1971-75; thirty-ninth president, 1977-*

A dark horse from the Deep South, Jimmy Carter made his swift and surprising entry on the national scene in 1976. Campaigning vigorously in all 50 states, the 51-year-old peanut farmer from Georgia promised to restore decency, candor, and compassion in government. "Trust me," he told the people time and again. "I will never lie to you..." The first Annapolis graduate, he was also the first Southerner in more than 100 years to assume the world's most powerful office.

His unusual career had its beginning in Georgia, his birthplace and home, a village of 6̲6̲ the peach and pecan country 100 odd miles sou of Atlanta.

In his boyhood he had known the rural poverty of the South in the Great Depression. "While I was growing up, there was no running water in our house," he recounted. "No inside toilet. I knew what it was to work in the fields, the hardest kind of work..." While in high school, Jimmy also worked in the family's peanut warehouse. He wrote out a detailed schedule of things to be done each day, and faithfully kept his schedule—an exercise in self-discipline which became habitual and served him well.

After his engineering studies at Georgia Tech, he resolved to get into Annapolis. He did so in 1947, doing graduate work in nuclear physics. "My earliest ambition was to go to Annapolis and eventually become Chief of Naval Operations." He became a top aide to Admiral Hyman Rickover, the builder of the first atomic-powered submarine, the *Nautilus,* and father of the nuclear navy. Young Carter idolized Admiral Rickover and took him for his model of the executive. "He was unbelievably hardworking and competent," Carter recorded. "He demanded total dedication from his subordinates. We feared and respected him and strove to please him..." Carter helped develop the new submarine program and, while in the Navy, served around the world, including the Far East.

Before entering the Navy, he had met and courted a blue-eyed brunette, Rosalynn Smith; they were married in 1946, when she was 19 and Carter, 22, and she became a Navy wife. Carter's father died in 1953, and they returned to Plains, Carter resigning from the Navy to run the family peanut business. Rosalynn kept the books. There were difficulties at the start. "When I got out of the Navy, with a wife and small children, I had no place to live," Carter recalled in a campaign speech. "I had no money, except some war bonds. So we moved into a public housing project. My rent was $28 a month... I know the importance of public housing."

Applying himself diligently to the peanut business, in the next ten years Carter made it prosper. "He was able to turn that peanut business from a nickel-and-dime operation into a multimillion-dollar operation," one observer noted. Carter entered local politics in 1962 and was elected state senator at the age of 38. In the Georgia legislature he read every bill, or from 800 to 1000 bills each session.

In 1966, he entered the race for the governorship of Georgia—and lost: a major crisis in his career. "When I failed at something, it was a horrible experience for me," he confessed later. Always a devout Baptist, he went through a period of self-searching which deepened his religious beliefs. The crisis enabled him to develop "an intimate personal relationship with God" and a new sense of inner peace. In this, he was helped by talks with his elder sister, Ruth Stapleton, a faith healer.

Carter ran for the governorship again in 1970, and won. His wife Rosalynn, serving on a commission, helped to set up a statewide network of mental health centers. His mother, Miss Lillian, a strong-willed matriarch with long experience as a nurse, had volunteered for the Peace Corps in 1967, at the age of 68, and was serving in India... Opinions on Carter as governor, by those who knew him in that office, were varied. "He has a mania for punctuality," said one observer. "He's obsessed with efficiency," said another. "He's moralistic . . . humorless . . . uncompromising." His personal secretary for six years noted: "The Governor is a very hard man to know." His younger brother Billy remarked: "What he really cares about are his religion and his children and machinery—to tinker with it and find out how it works... He's the smartest human being I've ever known."

In his carefully planned campaign for the White House, Carter wooed support from all quarters, reiterating his promise to restore to the presidency "all that is good and decent and honest and truthful and fair and competent and compassionate about the American people." Representing a new breed of the progressive Southerner, he promised to put blacks and women in his cabinet, and a woman on the Supreme Court. He held the support of the blacks. In Plains, he had been the only man who had refused to join the White Citizens' Council. While governor, he had appointed blacks to important posts in Georgia. His young daughter Amy went to an integrated school where the majority of students were black.

"Our country has lived through a time of torment. It's now a time for healing," Carter said in his acceptance speech at the Democratic Convention in New York. "We *can* have an America that has turned away from scandal and corruption and official cynicism... a president who's not isolated from the people but who feels your pain and shares your dreams and takes his strength and courage from you..."

In his campaign autobiography, Carter introduced himself as "a Southerner, and an American," in that order. He described himself as "an average person, no more complicated or enigmatic than others, but sensitive, tough, and a good planner." In the spring of 1976 in a candid television interview, Carter was questioned about his religious beliefs, and he remarked: "Although I've prayed a good bit, I've never asked God to let me be president...I ask God to let me do what's right and let me do what's best, that my life may be meaningful...I feel that I have one life to live and that God wants me to do the best I can with it."

After a decade of disappointment, marked by Viet-

nam and Watergate, the country turned to the smiling newcomer from Georgia and gave him its vote of fresh hope and confidence. Preparing to take the helm, Carter promised quick action on a broad national health plan, aid to cities, tax reform, welfare reform, tougher antitrust laws, housecleaning in government. He promised new long-range policies in agriculture, education, energy. In foreign affairs, he put the stress on human rights and called for the rigorous control of arms sales to repressive governments. He advocated joint action with allies, in economic fields, to enable democracies to lead the way "to a more just and more stable world order." With this program, Jimmy Carter won a close election in November, 1976, and became the thirty-ninth president of the United States.

So in 1976, as if to cap the Bicentennial, two centuries after the Declaration of Independence—and more than a century after the Civil War—America chose a man from the Deep South for its highest honor and most powerful office.

*President-elect Carter waving to his supporters and claiming victory in the Bicentennial presidential election of 1976*